REA

YOUR WEDDING

YOUR WAY

S0-BVO-212

YOUR WEDDING
YOUR WAY

LEAH INGRAM

AUTHOR OF *The Portable Wedding Consultant*

CB

CONTEMPORARY BOOKS

Library of Congress Cataloging-in-Publication Data

Ingram, Leah.
    Your wedding your way / Leah Ingram.
        p.   cm.
    Includes index.
    ISBN 0-8092-2526-3
    1. Wedding etiquette.   2. Weddings—Planning.   I. Title.
BJ2051.I54   2000
395.2'2—dc21   99-28739
                                         CIP

Cover design by Kim Bartko
Back cover photo by Sardi Klein
Interior design by Amy Yu Ng

Published by Contemporary Books
A division of NTC/Contemporary Publishing Group, Inc.
4255 West Touhy Avenue, Lincolnwood (Chicago), Illinois 60712-1975 U.S.A.

Printed in the United States of America
International Standard Book Number: 0-8092-2526-3
00 01 02 03 04 05 QB 20 19 18 17 16 15 14 13 12 11 10 9 8 7 6 5 4 3 2

To my husband, Bill Behre, and my two daughters, Jane and Anne. Without them, life would not be worth living.

CONTENTS

ACKNOWLEDGMENTS

I love writing about weddings. It is an extremely happy time in a couple's life, and I love being able to help men and women as they plan their new life together. But I couldn't offer such great advice in this book, or any of my other books, if it weren't for the hundreds of real-life brides and grooms who have shared their anecdotes with me. While my own wedding was a unique event, providing more than enough fodder for the books and articles I write, I love hearing the interesting and unusual ways other people personalize their weddings. Many of the anecdotes appearing in *Your Wedding Your Way* come from the creative couples who sent me E-mails about their weddings. Since there are too many of you to name, I'll just say "Thank you." I couldn't have written this book without you.

One of the ways I tracked down many of the brides and grooms I interviewed for this book was through professional organizations, associations, and services that I have used on a day-to-day basis in my life as a journalist and editor. My thanks to the American Society of Journalists and Authors' listserve and its private forum on CompuServe as well as Profnet service for helping me find great people with great wedding stories to share. These services also helped me find experts to interview and book authors to speak to who could offer relevant information for my book.

In addition, thanks to all my friends and family who put me in touch with people they knew who had unique weddings.

I can't forget to thank Betsy Lancefield, my editor at Contemporary Books, who was always there for me when I had questions about how I should approach a topic or whether the name of a chapter made sense. If it weren't for Betsy—and the fact that she almost instantaneously replied to all my cries for help with an E-mail—I don't think I could have put together such a great book.

Also responsible for helping me get this book done is my husband, Bill Behre. He was my external conscience when I was slacking off and was a good sounding board for ideas. He was also a great baby-sitter and I'm grateful for all the kid-wrangling he did when I had to meet my deadline.

INTRODUCTION

I'm one of the lucky ones. I can look back on my wedding without a pang of regret from wishing I'd done something differently. The way my husband and I got married and how we celebrated our union was definitely a wedding our way.

If only all brides and grooms could say the same. One of the most common complaints I hear from couples I speak to is that they wish they had had more say in the wedding they planned. If it isn't a bossy mother making decisions for them, it's the status quo that they feel they must live up to.

This book is designed to give you the power, inspiration, and ideas to plan your wedding your way. Forget what convention tells you to do. This is your day and you should have a wedding that truly reflects who you two are as a couple. Of course, I don't mean have a naked wedding because you are nudists. You do have to draw the line somewhere to accommodate your own needs and desires without completely excluding your parents' wishes or what your guests will appreciate and enjoy. The key is planning a wedding that you'll look back on fondly for years to come, without an ounce of regret.

Caveat Emptor

No wedding book would be complete without a bit of "buyer beware" advice. That is, you have to be a smart shopper while you plan your wedding. Unless you plan events for a living, you'll find your wedding to be a crash course in site selection, price haggling, and contract negotiation because you didn't know better. This book can help you become a savvy consumer so, against all odds, you won't get ripped off.

Here is some basic advice for finding and using the best vendors for your wedding. This advice applies to everyone, from the boutique where you'll buy your wedding dress to the baker who'll make your wedding cake.

• Find out about a business through word of mouth. Ask your friends, relatives, and coworkers for names of services and vendors they used at their weddings. Who are the ones they can't stop raving about? Get their phone numbers and call them.

• Visit a company's place of business, if at all possible, before hiring that company. You want to get a firsthand sense of how this person runs his or her business. If an office or shop is in total disarray, there's a chance that business is in such a state most of the time. Not that geniuses aren't messy, but you don't want to deal with a company that is so disorganized that they may forget to show up at your wedding or meet an important deadline.

• Once you've found a business you like, ask for more references—even if the business comes highly recommended from one person you know. You want to talk to at least two other brides, grooms, or families who've used this company in a similar capacity to how you'll be using it. Ask your references if the company showed up on time, behaved professionally, charged what they said they were going to charge, etc. Ask them what they would have changed or done differently if they had the chance to hire this company again.

• After you've checked references, call the government. Check with your local Better Business Bureau or state attorney general to see if any disgruntled customers have lodged complaints against the company. Find out if those complaints were resolved. While there are some consumers who notoriously complain about what they perceive as bad service—and potentially tarnish the image of a company who really did its job fine—what you want to look for is a history of unresolved complaints. If a company has ignored previous customer complaints, then you can't be sure that this company will treat you right.

• Get everything in writing. If you're ordering a dress and they promise that the dress will arrive on April 1, have someone write that on your sales slip and sign it. When you find a bandleader that you like, put his or her name on the contract you sign with the company so you're guaranteed that the person you want shows up for the job. With vendors who will be coming to your ceremony or reception, make sure you put in writing the time they are to show up, how they are to be dressed, and how long you expect them to be on the clock. Also put in writing, especially for vendors at the reception, how many (if any) breaks they'll get and whether or not you'll be expected to feed them.

• Pay by credit card. If a company doesn't have the ability to take credit cards, let him or her know that you'll be taking your business elsewhere. Many couples who are trying to manage their finances prefer to pay for everything in cash or by check so they won't incur any additional debt. But for *your* wedding, you want to pay for everything by credit card. First, this way you have a bona fide record of the transaction (i.e., a credit card statement). And, second, if the company doesn't come through for you as promised, you have the credit card company to back you up. That is, you can dispute the charges on your statement, and the credit card company will help investigate the nonservice. In the meantime, you won't have to pay the disputed charges, and you won't incur any finance charges or late fees on the amount in dispute.

• Go with your gut feeling. If after all the checking around and calling references you still feel that a certain company isn't right for you, then don't hire it. I'm a big believer in going with a gut feeling, and I like to believe I'm a savvy consumer and smart shopper because I listen to what my instincts tell me. The last thing you want on your wedding day is to feel ripped off. This is supposed to be one of the happiest days of your life. If you approach it like a conscientious consumer, it most definitely will be.

Your Wedding
Your Way

BEYOND BLACK AND WHITE

What's walking down the aisle at today's modern wedding? Along with the traditional wedding gowns and formal tuxedos, brides and grooms are using their wedding attire to state their individualities. Brides are choosing gowns in anything but white and wearing dresses with interesting silhouettes. Their grooms are sporting unique ties with tuxedos or shucking the tuxedo altogether and wearing nontraditional suits.

When we got married, my husband wore khakis, a blue oxford shirt, a floral tie, and a navy blazer to our wedding. Like him, I hardly followed tradition when choosing my wedding attire. Did I make an appointment at the well-known New York bridal gown mecca, Kleinfeld's? No way. Did I visit the couture bridal salons on Manhattan's tony Madison Avenue? Of course not. And I even completely bucked tradition by buying my wedding gown *before* I was even engaged. Yes, you heard it right. I was a gal with a wedding dress but no place to wear it.

Actually, I wasn't as pathetic as I'm making myself sound. At the time, Bill and I were living together and were talking marriage. I just hadn't been officially asked, and there was no rock on the third finger from my thumb. So, according to snooty etiquette mavens, I wasn't officially engaged and had no right to go gown shopping. But did I listen to the little etiquette voices in my head? No way.

One sunny spring day I decided to check out the sales at Lord & Taylor department store. As I exited the escalator in the ladies dress department, I had an experience like something out of a movie. Music started playing in my head (perhaps it was harps), the aisles around me became dark, and a spotlight shone brightly on a display rack featuring ivory dresses. Before I knew it, I was moving toward the dress rack as if the floor had become one of the moving walkways you find in airports.

The dress before me was the most beautiful garment I'd ever seen. It was a three-quarters-length dress with a dropped waist. The sleeves were capped and the bodice featured the most delicate embroidery. Also enhancing the dress's inherent beauty were tiny pearlized buttons that ran the length of the dress, from the scooped neck to the hem. I just had to try it on. I practically floated to the dressing room.

Even though my legs were unshaven and my pale, pasty winter face had not a speck of makeup on (nor did my finger bear the aforementioned requisite ring), I felt radiant in the dress and I knew it was *the* dress for me. I had to buy it. I got dressed, paid for the dress (about $150), and bounded out of the store into the sunshine. I was ecstatic. Now I had to break the news to Bill. He took it in stride, as he does with most of the goofy things I do in our life. However, now that I had my dress, I had to get him to ask me to marry him so I wouldn't look like a complete idiot having a wedding gown hanging in my closet and no wedding date to speak of. Lucky for me, Bill is a good guy (that's why I eventually married him) and he popped the question soon thereafter. While I wouldn't suggest that most women go out and buy their wedding dresses before they get engaged, the point is you've got to buy the wedding dress that speaks to you, if you will, the way my dress spoke to me.

✎ *Doing It Her Way* ✎

"The first day I started looking for my wedding dress, I went into a dressy dress shop, told the salesperson there that I was getting married for the second time, that I didn't have the slightest idea what I wanted, but that I'd know it when I saw the dress. The owner looked me over, went to the rack, looked for a minute and took out one dress. As soon as I saw it, I knew it was exactly right.

"The dress of my dreams ended up being a pink lace over-slip dress, which was regular length in front but about ten inches longer in the back. It came with a matching pink satin blousey jacket. I paid less than $250 for the dress.

"We went on a cruise a week after the wedding. So before we left, I had my dress cleaned and took it along on the cruise, to wear for one of the formal nights. No one knew it was my wedding gown. The best part is this dress has had a life long after my wedding. I've subsequently had the hem evened out and I wear it for weddings and other formal events."

—*Ellen, East Setauket, New York*

A New Hue for You

It is very important you wear a wedding gown that reflects who you are. For example, if the bride is an executive, wears tailored suits to work every day, and loves the buttoned-up look, then it would make perfect sense for her to wear a form-fitting wedding gown, such as some of the body-skimming gowns designers have debuted lately. Someone who looks polished every day of the week probably would feel like her wedding was a total sham if she tied the knot wearing something from Bo Peep's closet. Likewise, a creative bride who works in advertising, graphic design, or another artistic field isn't going to go for the same old wedding gown. She may choose to wear her grandmother's vintage wedding gown or a new gown with a unique design in anything but white or ivory. Lucky for her, some designers have recently debuted gowns in such shocking hues as platinum, canary yellow, or pale blue and in shapes anything but ordinary. One New York designer recently showed wedding gowns with an exposed midriff (start working on your abs now).

Take Darcy of New York City as an example of a truly modern bride. Darcy, a visual artist, says that as a child she always dreamed of getting married in Morticia Addams's dress, except instead of black, she envisioned her dream dress in red. Guess what she wore when she tied the knot a few years

Traditions with a Twist

Brides who decide that a tinted wedding gown is right for them may wonder what to do with their bridesmaids' dresses. How about dressing them in white? One bride who wore a blush pink gown had her four bridesmaids wear white dresses—the color combination looked stunning.

ago? "A deep, burgundy red velvet gown that I purchased in a shop that re-creates antique dresses," she recalls. "The pattern for the gown was derived from a 1930s dress. I also wore deep-red silk shoes. For me, the color symbolizes passionate love."

Obviously, Darcy was way ahead of the trend away from pure white wedding dresses. Look through a bridal magazine today, and while most of the pages feature white gowns, you'll see new hues sneaking in here and there. A recent issue of *Modern Bride* highlighted gowns in copper, silver, and pale pink.

Whether you decide to buy a gown in a funky color or something more traditional, you have to understand exactly the process of buying a wedding gown. You have two choices: buy off the rack or buy a custom dress.

Buying off the Rack

When you buy off the rack, this means that you're buying the very dress you try on, like I did. You've got a couple of choices when you buy off the rack (which is why it's my favorite way of buying a dress). But don't let my preferences stop you from having a custom-made wedding gown, if after reading this chapter you decide that that is the best option for you.

Visit a department store. Do not stop at the bridal boutique. Do not pass "Go." Head directly for the evening-wear department where you'll

1 Do Data

Of wedding dress preferences, most brides (73 percent) prefer white, 39 percent wear a traditional ball gown, and 56 percent choose a dress made of satin, according to the Association of Bridal Consultants.

find many gowns that a bride could wear—in very bridal colors, such as white and ivory. And here's the good part: because these lovely dresses are sold as formal wear (remember: you're not in the so-called bridal section of the store), they cost a lot less than a wedding gown would. Better yet, because women of all sizes need to go to a formal affair at some time, evening wear is sold in a range of sizes—as opposed to most wedding gowns, which are made for someone who has a body like Cindy Crawford's. When you go to a bridal boutique, however, unless you wear a size 8 or size 10 (and plenty of you do, but I don't, so I can get a bit

---

Traditions with a Twist

If you'd like to wear a traditional white or ivory wedding gown, but don't want to pay big bucks for a fancy dress, check out bridesmaid dresses or those sold as prom dresses. Many are made by the very manufacturers who do wedding gowns, and they offer styles that look very "bridal," if you will. Best of all, you can get what is supposed to be a bridesmaid or prom dress in white or ivory, call it your wedding dress, and pay only a couple hundred bucks. In fact, on a recent trip to the mall, I noticed a bevy of dresses in the junior department that looked like wedding dresses. My first thought was whether or not this national retailer was promoting the concept of underage brides. Then I looked closer and realized that these so-called wedding gowns were actually prom dresses. You could have fooled me!

---

snippy about it at times), you can't actually try your dress on until your order comes in. But more about that later.

If you are a size 8 or size 10, check out the sales at a bridal boutique. Before you walk in the door, understand that you are there to check out only the off-the-rack sales. You are not there to begin trying on this season's hottest dresses. You can save that for another day if you decide the off-the-rack thing doesn't work for you. Instead, tell the overly helpful salesperson that you would like to see any of last season's leftovers. Don't be shocked when you see what she brings you. Because these dresses have been through an entire year's worth of trying on, they may be a little dirty and perhaps a bit worn. Don't worry. A professional dry cleaner can get your dress back in tip-top shape. In the meantime, use your best judgment to see through the grime. You just might find your dream dress in this pile of leftovers. And, it won't cost as much as it did when it was considered "current."

Another great source for off-the-rack dresses are resale or consignment shops that feature "gently used" dresses. This is where rich people unload their worldly possessions, including wedding dresses that were worn only once (one hopes) and are probably in perfect condition. One consignment shop I know of on Manhattan's Upper East Side is filled with the cast-off dresses from New York's social elite. These dresses are nothing to sneeze at. They're made by such top designers as Vera Wang, Oscar de la Renta, and Christian Dior and look brand-new. Because "real" people wore them once, the dresses come in a range of sizes, not just a sample size. Here's the best part: some of the original owners paid upward of $5,000 for these frocks. But because these dresses are no longer considered brand-new, customers rarely pay more than $1,500. (Fifteen hundred dollars—that's a lot of money. It is, and if you can afford to

I Do Data

According to the Wedding Trends 1999 survey from *Bridal Guide* magazine, women spend, on average, $991 for their wedding gown.

spend that much on a dress, you may prefer to be the *first* person to wear that kind of dress. Therefore, skip directly to the section on custom dresses. This resale shop thing may not be for you.)

Besides getting their stock from people who need to clean out their closets, many resale and consignment shops get their inventory from dress designers who want to unload excess dresses and get a tax write-off (many resale shops benefit charitable causes). If you buy your dress at a place like this, you can feel good about your little shopping spree because your purchase will help support a good cause. Also you may be able to convince your accountant to include the receipt from your dress purchase as a charitable donation. But check with your accountant first. (I'm a wedding expert; I *don't* give out IRS-related advice.)

To find a consignment or resale shop near you, look in the Yellow Pages under "consignment shops" or use the words "consignment" or "resale" when searching the Web. Because sizes may be limited at stores where the primary source of dresses is designers (as opposed to regular people who wear a variety of sizes), call first to find out where a store gets its stock. If you're a size 2 or a size 12 but all a resale store stocks are size 8s or size 10s, obviously you'll want to shop elsewhere.

Check out discounters, bridal outlets, or sample sales. One such store is Tati in New York City, which makes its money by buying the end lots (leftovers) from bridal designers. Because the dresses are past their prime (meaning they're from last season), the designers want to get them off their hands fast. They sell them in large volume and for a small price tag to stores like Tati, which then pass the savings along to the customer. "We sell dresses that would have retailed for $2,400 for only $400," explains Tati owner Ilyse Wilpon. "Sure, you can say they're last season's dresses, but people wear their grandmother's dress," so what does it mat-

➤ Doing It Her Way ➤

"For my Valentine's Day wedding, I wore my mother's wedding gown, but with a twist. My mother, a size 8, had worn a form-fitting ivory satin gown with cap sleeves and a massive hoop. I was devastated when my size 14 body wouldn't squeeze into her dress. But then I got an idea. I thought there might be some hope: because there was so much material in the skirt, maybe we could use it to alter the dress. (Mom's hoop was so big that her dad and her attendants had to squeeze the bottom and sides of it in so she could fit down the aisle of the church!) I found a designer who was able to retain the basic style of the gown but use the extra fabric to make the dress fit me. Needless to say, I felt immense pride in being able to wear my mother's gown." —*Sue, Ewing, New Jersey*

ter *when* the dress was modern? "The key is does it fit and do you love it?" (A $2,400 dress at $2,000 off? I could love that any day!)

You have to have a certain amount of patience and perseverance if you decide to go the outlet route. Most outlets are housed in warehouse-type spaces and the accoutrements are kept to a bare minimum. Don't expect any comfy couches to rest upon or elegantly appointed dressing rooms with salespeople bringing you bottled water. Instead, be prepared to face row after row of dresses, arranged either by size or price tag. Dressing rooms at outlets usually amount to a draped off corner of a room, so leave your bashful self at home.

It's best to bring at least two people with you. That way one person can hold any dresses you're considering—if you put them down, someone else could snatch them—and another can fetch things for you after you've staked out a place in the dressing room. That's what Susan of Portsmouth, Virginia, did when she visited the Bridal Mart Wearhouse (*sic*) in Burlington, North Carolina. She enlisted her mother, aunt, and cousin to help her in her quest to find her affordable dream gown. In fact, the quest for affordable gowns is what drove Susan and family to travel four hours to this place, buzzing with brides on a Saturday afternoon.

Susan explains: "I found the dress of my dreams in a bridal magazine. It was perfect and exactly what I'd dreamed about—until I found out the price: $1,790. I contacted twenty-five seamstresses and almost hired one to make the dress, but even that would have cost $700." Then Susan found an ad for the Bridal Mart Wearhouse in one of her bridal magazines and decided it was worth checking out. Maybe her dream dress would be there, and it wouldn't cost nearly $1,800. She brought along the page that pictured the gown she loved. "After trying on seven beautiful gowns, none of them measured up to the one dress I wanted," Susan recalls. "As I was about to start crying, my aunt handed me a gown and said, 'This kind of looks like the one in the picture. Do you want to try it on?' It was *the* dress, only it was made by a different manufacturer. And the price tag was better than great: $247!"

The only problem: it was the wrong size and the wrong color. But all hope wasn't lost. Susan asked one

1 Do Data

Most brides spend ten months, on average, looking for a wedding gown. According to the Association of Bridal Consultants, the average number of dresses a bride will actually try on before finding the dress she buys is 12.5, and most brides (45.5 percent) will buy their dresses on sale.

⤞ News You Can Use: Using the Web ⤝

"The Web is great for planning a wedding because there's so much you can do while sitting at your computer," says Lisa Price, coauthor of *The Best of Online Shopping: The Prices' Guide to Fast and Easy Shopping on the Web* (Ballantine, 1999), which includes advice on how to find wedding-related services via the Web. "Why schlepp to several bridal boutiques when you can see three times the number of dresses on-line in a fraction of the time?" she wonders. (Well, if you're like me and want to touch and feel every article of clothing you buy, down to your socks, then buying a dress over the Web may not be for you. But it's a great place to get started.)

"What bride-to-be doesn't pour through the bridal magazines, looking for the perfect bridal gown?" Price adds. "Then when she finds it in the magazine, she can't find it in the stores." Price recommends checking out All Bridal Attire (http://members.aol.com/allbridal), which offers a nifty feature. You can type in the name of the magazine where you saw a dress along with the page and the date—and they'll let you know if they can get it, she says.

"Some Web stores serve as mini wedding malls," Price continues. "Discount Designer Bridal Gowns (www.thebridalshoppe.com) has over five hundred wedding gowns and bridesmaid dresses from almost every major designer—at discount prices. They also sell mother's dresses, headpieces, shoes, slips, bras, jewelry, and, for the groom, tuxedos."

❧ Doing It Her Way ❧

"When I began searching for my wedding gown, I knew I wanted something very simple and chic. My mother and I went to the Vera Wang boutique in New York City, where every gown looked and felt beautiful—but at $5,000 to $8,000 apiece, they were out of my price range. We then decided to try our local bridal store, but after Vera Wang, every gown seemed cheap by comparison. Feeling desperate, I continued my search.

"The next week, a friend came running into my office with a copy of *New York Magazine.* She had just read that Vera Wang was holding a sample sale that Saturday at a local hotel. Of course, I had to go.

"My mother and I arrived at 9:00 A.M. and waited in line for two hours before we finally got in. We thought all the dresses would be gone by then, but we discovered that there were still racks and racks of beautiful dresses.

"I tried on at least fifty dresses. Some were dirty, some ripped, some were perfect. We had narrowed it down to two dresses when we saw a girl trying on a dress that was perfect. But it seemed like she was going to take it. My mom asked her, if she decided she didn't want the dress, to please give it to us. And you know what? She did.

"The dress was perfect. Not only was it beautiful—it had a silk bodice, organza skirt, and simple beading on the sleeves and waist—but it had never been used as a sample, so it was still in its protective plastic cover. And the price was right. The dress retailed for more than $5,500 and we got it for $1,500."

—Dina, Westfield, New Jersey

of the salespeople if she could help, and it turned out that they would order Susan a brand-new dress, in the right size and color, and still only charge her $247. Not only did Susan save $1,543 on her dress, but the store was also having a shoe sale, whereby brides who bought dresses got a free pair of shoes. "Within ten minutes of finding my dream dress, we'd put down a half payment (the balance was to be paid when we received the dress), picked out my free shoes, and we were on our way," Susan recalls.

Brides looking to have a similar shopping experience to Susan's should check out ads in bridal magazines, look in the Yellow Pages, or use the Web to track down various discounters. Best yet, sometimes discounters list their dress prices right on their websites. This way you can do some comparison shopping without leaving the comfort of your home (or your office, if you happen to be planning your wedding on company time, as so many of today's busy brides do). I wouldn't recommend buying a dress over the Web, however. You really want to try your gown on before laying down any cash.

The one drawback to buying from a discounter is you often can't tell who made your dress because it won't have its original label in it. That's probably because most manufacturers don't want the word to get out that they are selling their gowns at a heavy discount.

If you live in or near New York City, sample sales can be a great way to find a wedding gown at a fraction of its original price. Check out the "Sales and Bargains" column in *New York Magazine* each week. (It's online at www.newyorkmag.com for those who don't live in the tri-state New York area.) When I was planning my wedding, I read this column and discovered a glove maker who was having a sample sale. Her hand-crocheted cotton gloves, which normally retail for more than $100, were being sold for about $20 each. I went to her cramped showroom and found two pairs of gloves that I loved and that looked great with my dress—one had tiny sunflowers embroidered around the edges. I ended up wearing that pair at my reception, and the gloves really brought my outfit together. Whatever happened to the other pair? I'm keeping it for my daughters to use as dress-up clothes.

If you decide to buy off-the-rack, understand that you'll have to handle any alterations yourself, and sometimes it's hard to find a seamstress who knows how to work with delicate dresses. Therefore, you should ask the salespeople at the store whom they would recommend, and ask your friends as well. Getting a personal referral is the best way to find someone you can trust to take in or let out your dress.

While discounters, outlets, and samples sales make a lot of sense for bargain hunters, if you're really into labels (you make sure everyone sees the Kate Spade name on your handbag and your license plate says something like KIMSBMW), you may want to go the traditional route in shopping for your gown. If you'll get off on being able to say "Well, when I went shopping for my Vera Wang gown" and "Yes, my Kenneth Cole shoes matched my Vera Wang gown perfectly" then go ahead and make an appointment to visit Vera Wang. She makes gorgeous gowns, and you won't regret spending a few weeks' salary on the perfect wedding dress for you, if

I Do Data

The Association of Bridal Consultants says that the top three headpiece choices are a tiara, wreath, and headband. A bride will spend, on average, $171 on her headpiece.

that's what you want to do for this once-in-a-lifetime (one would hope) dress.

Buying a Custom Gown

Buying a custom dress means just as it sounds—you're buying a dress made specially for you. You could have a dress made from scratch by an entrepreneur who specializes in designing one-of-a-kind dresses. Or, you could do what thousands of brides do each year: go to a traditional bridal boutique to buy their wedding gown. The catch is you don't walk out with the dress of your dreams; it has to be ordered and then fitted—you won't have the finished product for about six months.

If you decide that this option is the best way for you to find the dress that reflects who you are, then the various wedding magazines on the newsstand will become your best friends. You won't even have to worry about working out at the gym; you'll be getting your biceps, pecs, and deltoids in shape for a sleeveless wedding gown (if you choose to wear one) simply from carrying around issues of bridal magazines—they sometimes weigh in at more than five pounds each! Besides the traditional bridal books (*Brides, Modern Bride, Bridal Guide,* and *Elegant Bride*), there are a ton of local and national magazines that have special wedding sections. Check these out for advertisements and editorial write-ups about local businesses and to see fashion spreads on what's hot on the wedding runway.

The best way to prepare yourself for the long walk down the wedding-gown shopping aisle is to take to tearing your wedding magazines apart—not because of frustration but because you'll want to keep the pictures of dresses that you like. (I suggest buying a folder or notebook in which to keep all your wedding-related research, including ads for dresses.) When you look at these dresses, it's okay to go with your fantasy (dress like Princess Di, husband like Tom Cruise, but I digress) and pull out dresses that are completely out there. But you've got to keep your own body in mind and stay away from dresses that are unflattering to it. For example, if you're sensitive about the size of your hips, a dress with a fitted bodice that explodes into a poufy tulle skirt (think Glinda the Good Witch from *The Wizard of Oz*) is probably a really bad option for you.

Understanding ahead of time which dresses will look good on you and which won't will help you once you actually start going to bridal stores to try on dresses—well, if you can actually try anything on. Unfortunately, as I said earlier, many of these shops stock samples in sizes 8 or 10. So, unless you wear that size, you'll either have to hold a dress up to your body to see if you like it, or if you're petite, you can try it on but, obviously, it's going to be too big. (Note: Please don't take this policy of the bridal gown manufacturers as your carte blanche to go on a crash diet so you'll be a size 8 or size 10 for your dress-buying days. Your fiancé is marrying you for who you are, not for a size that a manufacturer believes a bride should be. It's simply easier for dress designers to send a limited number of sizes to stores; even if it might seem like it, it isn't a subversive plot from Weight Watchers!)

Anyway, here is where your bridesmaids, mother, and good friends become crucial to you. If you bring them along on your dress-buying expeditions (and I highly recommend that you do), you can do an ersatz fashion show for them, even if it means holding a dress up to your body. Together, you can use your imaginations to determine if a dress gets a thumbs up or a thumbs down.

Once you find the dress you love—and it is possible even without trying something on and having it fit—then a seamstress will take your measurements, you'll place an order for your dress (and give a down payment), and then you probably won't hear anything for three or four months until your dress comes in. At that time, you'll have to go through a bevy of fittings to get the length right (most dresses are cut for a woman standing five foot nine), to make sure the bodice fits you properly, and to make sure the sleeves are the proper length (rolling up the sleeves of your wedding gown is not cool).

After all these alterations are made, you'll come back for a second fitting, at which point your dress will be done. You will be extremely ecstatic by now. Just because your dress is complete, however, doesn't mean you should take it home. One great thing about a bridal boutique is that the staff knows how to take care of bridal gowns, including pressing them and keeping them clean. So, your dress will stay in perfect condition until the day you need it. In fact, I would highly recommend that you leave your dress at the boutique until the day before your wedding. (Get your maid of honor to pick it up for you so you don't have to worry about running around and doing last-minute errands.) Why do you want to leave picking up your dress until the last minute? One Colorado bridal boutique owner recalls the bride who brought her dress home early and laid it out on her bed so she could admire it, only to have her cat decide it was the perfect replacement for its litter box.

Of course, leaving your dress at the boutique until the last minute seems like a huge leap of faith. You may be thinking "What if they go out of business before my wedding?" This question is exactly why, before you buy a dress from a store, you want to call the Better Business Bureau and your state's attorney general's office and check the place out. Both offices take consumer complaints and will have on record whether or not customers have been dissatisfied with the service they received from the business. (Note: You should check the Better Business Bureau and attorney general's office before hiring *any* business for your wedding, as I said in the Introduction.)

A few years back, I went with my friend Carla when she was looking for a wedding gown. She had considered shopping at one store whose name popped up over and over in all the dress ads in bridal magazines. It just happened that the night before our appointment, the local news did a story on wedding scams. The store we were supposed to visit the next day led the story. They were notorious for making brides pay in full up front (most stores ask for a deposit and then payment in full when the dress arrives) and then making brides wait weeks, even months, longer than anticipated for their dresses. The store in question made one bride whom the television station interviewed wait so long that she ended up having to go to another store and pay rush charges to get her wedding dress in time for her ceremony. Needless to say, Carla and I did not visit that store. Instead, we hissed at it when we drove by on our way to the more reputable store, where Carla ended up buying her wedding dress.

Great Groom's Attire

Not surprisingly, figuring out what your fiancé is going to wear to the wedding is a lot easier than determining what your dress is going to look like. Guys really do have it easier. It'll be a tux or a suit. Period. End of story. Luckily, sky-blue leisure suits never made it back into fashion, so

~~✄ *Doing It Her Way* ✄~~

"Our wedding was a variation on the 'tuxes and tennis shoes' theme. We invited our wedding party to wear sneakers to the wedding, and many of them did. Mike and I wore them as well. He wore black Nike sneakers, and I wore a pair of funky white tennis shoes, with chunky heels (very 90s-style). To dress them up a bit, I replaced the laces with iridescent lace, organza ribbon. Oh, and I added a blue satin bow on the back of the sneaker as my 'something blue.'"

—*Susan, Portsmouth, Virginia*

you needn't worry about your guy requesting something like that. (If he does, what will you do?) However, short of making a fashion faux pas, you do have a little bit of room for creativity, if you so choose, in the groom's attire. Here are some ideas on how your guy's personality can shine through his wedding attire:

• Sneak something a little off-beat into his tuxedo ensemble. One bride I know who is a big Elvis freak convinced her husband-to-be to wear a matching tie and cummerbund that looked like blue suede. If you're going for a true black-and-white wedding, you may want your fiancé to wear a black shirt with his black tuxedo for a different look.

• Don't let him wear just a basic bow tie. According to formal dress wear shops, one of the hottest ties today is called a four-in-hand tie that looks like a cross between a traditional business tie and an ascot.

• Think vests. What's great about a vest is that even when a groom takes off his jacket, he still looks dressed. Vests are a neat way to slip some fun into the groom's attire, too. Many manufacturers offer reversible vests. One side looks traditional, but the other side may feature the logo of your fiancé's favorite football team, his alma mater's mascot, or a sea of smiley faces. Have him show the serious side of the vest under his tuxedo jacket during the ceremony, and then he can switch sides during the reception.

• When in doubt, a great suit will do. It isn't written in stone anywhere that a man must get married in a tuxedo. In fact, according to etiquette mavens, tuxedos should only be worn for evening weddings, and something called a morning suit (think *Four Weddings and a Funeral*) should be worn for a morning or afternoon wedding. However, today's brides and grooms can get away with anything they want. Personally, I think a tailored navy or grey suit looks as nice, if not better, than a tuxedo (I can't help but picture penguins).

If you're getting married in an exotic locale (see Chapter 9, "Weddings Away") or eloping (see Chapter 10, "To Elope or Not to Elope: That Is the Question"), disregard all this advice and do whatever you want.

Your Way or No Way

Before you head out to the stores to buy your wedding gown, keep the following in mind; it may just help you keep your sanity, too.

❦ Keep your options open. If you think buying off-the-rack is the best option for you, make sure that along with looking at off-the-rack dresses you also visit at least one traditional bridal salon and look at dresses that must be custom ordered. You'll never know which kind of dress is going to jump out at you, grab you by the shoulders, and scream "You must buy me now!" It could be an off-the-rack number or it might be a custom gown.

❦ Bring along reinforcements. While it's okay to start dabbling in dress buying by yourself, it's best to bring along others for their opinions when you make your final decision. Too often in wedding planning, brides get so caught up in the image they want to create that they lose their common sense. That's why you want to have close friends, a sister (if you have one), or even your mother around to create a jury of peers. Then when you hold up the really ugly dress, which under normal circumstances you would have sneered at but are now salivating over, they can bring you back to reality by giving you the thumbs down in unison.

❦ Make an appointment before visiting a traditional bridal salon. While you may think that having to make an appointment to shop for dresses is *très snob*, it actually makes a ton of sense. By doing so you know that you'll have one salesperson who is dedicating her time to you—and only you. At some salons, however, the salesperson is so dedicated to you that she won't let you look at dresses unless she has picked them out for you first. So, if you're a tactile shopper who prefers touching and feeling a garment's fabric before trying it on—and you're a control freak—this method of gown shopping may make you a little nuts.

❦ Eat a little something beforehand. Don't scarf down an extra-large meal at a fast-food restaurant before your shopping expedition (you'll feel greasy and bloated). But at the same time, don't starve yourself so that your tummy will look flatter in the dresses. You need to eat for energy, and you have no idea how exhausting trying on dresses can be until three hours have passed, you're on dress number forty-five, and you still haven't found anything you like. Plus, you shouldn't starve yourself with the hopes of buying a dress that will fit a body that is ten pounds lighter. *Please* buy a dress that looks good on you *now*. The weeks and months leading up to the wedding are not the time to go on a diet. Love yourself for who you are and buy a dress that looks good on who you are now, not who you hope to be.

❦ Don't be afraid to buy the first dress you see or try on—or the dress you've always been dreaming about—if you totally fall in love with it once you actually see it in person. I'm a big believer in love at first sight. So is a bride I know—consider her anecdote.

When Chicago bride Marty was planning her wedding, "I was determined not to pay too much for a dress and not to get a dress that was too frilly," she recalls. "For several weeks I tried on every cheap suit, narrow skirt, and off-white dress devoid of beads or sparkles in the Chicago area." She found nothing to her liking.

Not surprisingly, Marty started to get a little depressed. Soon thereafter, she flew out to visit her sister in Williamsburg, Virginia, to help her pick out her bridesmaid dress. While waiting for her sister to come out of the dressing room at one of the stores they were visiting, Marty spied a rack of wedding gowns. "One of them was a full-length dress with a huge tulle skirt" (oh, no, the frill Marty wanted to avoid), but there was something about the dress that Marty liked. "It was completely hand-embroidered with green leaves and vines plus it was beaded with pink and white flowers." Sounds awful, right? But against what Marty thought was her better judgment, she tried the dress on. "Not only was it extraordinarily expensive, but it was completely frilly—and it fit me perfectly," she recalls.

Because Marty still thought her wedding dress should be non-frill, she didn't buy it. But for the next few weeks, she drove everyone crazy talking about the dress, including her fiancé, Steve. Or, at least she thought she was driving him crazy. Fast-forward a few months to Christmas morning, when in walks Steve with a huge box, and guess what was inside? Marty's dream dress. After all of Marty's incessant lamenting about not buying the dress, Steve called the shop, bought it for her, and had it shipped to their home. What a great guy!

2

Best Men and Women

When I found out my friend Donna was engaged, I couldn't wait for her to ask me to be in her wedding. Friends since we met at age four, at swimming lessons, we'd always promised that we would be each other's maid of honor. In college, Donna finally met the man she would marry, but she never asked me to be her maid of honor or even a bridesmaid.

I didn't make the bridesmaid cut in my friend Laura's wedding, either. Since Laura was my maid of honor, you would have thought that she would automatically include me in her wedding. But she didn't. Am I still speaking to both Laura and Donna? Of course, I am. Are they still my closest girlfriends? You bet. I love them both very much, even though I wasn't in their weddings.

Huh? you may be asking yourself. Aren't you angry? Sure, at first I was a bit hurt that I wasn't asked, but then they explained the criteria they each used for choosing attendants.

Donna's mother had died the year before she got married. In the time leading up to her mother's death (unfortunately prolonged cancer), Donna grew very close to her two sisters and her two brothers' wives, all of whom worked together to make Donna's mother as comfortable as possible at the end of her life. When Donna chose those four women to stand up at her wedding, I couldn't possibly be mad. I was very touched that she chose as her attendants the four women who were the closest and dearest to her at that point in her life.

Laura's situation was entirely different. When we were working together at a New York publishing company, Laura and I saw each other every day and often on weekends. Even after we took jobs at other companies, we still got together at least once a week for a meal or just to hang out. Soon after I got married, I moved to Michigan, where I lived for four years. While Laura and I talked fairly regularly over the phone and kept up our friendship that way, obviously things were different between us. Soon after I had my second child and moved back to the East Coast, Laura got engaged. While I would have been honored to have been in her wedding, I was secretly relieved when she didn't ask me. She later explained that since I was very busy writing books and taking care of two kids, she figured the last thing I wanted to do was spend money on a bridesmaid dress I'd never wear again. When she didn't ask me to be in her wedding—and explained why—I was thrilled that she had been so sensitive to my needs.

What mattered most to both Donna and Laura was that I could be there as a friend and guest when they both said "I do." And I was.

It is critical that you think long and hard about whom you want to be in your wedding before asking anyone to be an attendant. In the years since I started writing about weddings, I've heard about countless girls and guys who got so excited about being engaged that they asked anyone and everyone to be in their wedding party. Suddenly, they had forty attendants to manage. Maybe I'm exaggerating, but I have spoken with couples who didn't know how to un-ask someone to be in their wedding, after asking on impulse, and ended up with double-digit wedding parties. Try fitting twelve or fifteen people up on the altar or under a *huppah*. It isn't easy.

That's not to say that you shouldn't have eight bridesmaids or your fiancé shouldn't have nine groomsmen, especially if you come from a big family and want to include all eight of your siblings. However, the best way to choose attendants is to take a two-pronged approach. First, figure out who are the most meaningful people in your life, and second, determine who can afford and will want to be a part of your wedding. Also keep in mind that if you're planning a long engagement—over a year—hold off choosing attendants for as long as you can, especially if you're going to go with all friends and no family members. I say this because friendships can sometimes hit a speed bump—and cause your wedding plans to crash, especially if that person was going to be your maid of honor—whereas siblings will probably stick by you no matter what.

Take Susan of San Francisco, who chose a close friend from work to be her maid of honor. Over the year it took to plan Susan's wedding, however, her friendship with this woman started to wane. By the time the wedding rolled around, the two were barely talking to each other. "If I had the chance to do it all again, I would have chosen my attendants differently," says Susan regretfully. "I believe that if you are contemplating a family member over a friend as maid of honor or best man, more often than not, the sibling would be the best choice. A wedding is not only a union of two people but the union of two families." She says that a sibling understands better than a friend that a wedding can be a very stress-ful time for the bride and groom. "You can be yourself with your brother or sister, even when you're not behaving your best," Susan adds, "and because this is your sibling, you don't have to worry about the friendship ramifications."

While Susan's is a well-taken point, it may not be universally accepted. Elliot and Beatty Cohan, authors of *For Better, for Worse, Forever: 10 Steps for Building a Lasting Relationship with the Man You Love* (Chandler House Press, 1999), say that a true friend will be there for you as a bridesmaid and she'll be there for you even if she isn't in your wedding. "I think a wedding is a time when couples find out whether their friends are true friends," they say. "If a friend is hurt and not speaking to you because she wasn't made a bridesmaid, you have to ask yourself if this person truly was your friend. The true test of a friendship is not when things go well but when things start to go off track. That's when you find out what kind of friendship or relationship you have with a person."

Who Is Meaningful?

How do you figure out who are the most meaningful people to you? Start by listing the friends you see regularly and whose company you enjoy. Then ask yourself "Why is this person important to me?" suggests Elliot. Some friends tend to stand out more than others, explains Elliot, "because they represent some event or significant time in your life." For Brooke, a newlywed and recent college graduate in Los Angeles, her friends from college were her "dearest friends."

Before you go ahead and ask someone, Elliot suggests that you share your list of potential attendants with your future spouse. "The bride may want some friends of hers from the office, but the groom may not want to include them because he doesn't know them," he says. Sometimes it's best to choose attendants "that both [the bride and groom] are friendly with."

Doing so isn't very easy, as Tina and Bart of Boston learned when they were planning their wedding. "For starters, my husband and I had different ideas about what size the bridal party should be, as well as who should be included," Tina recalls. "If it were up to me, I would have had my best friends and my sisters—six attendants in all." Unfortunately for Tina, Bart vetoed one of Tina's selections—her friend Lisa. "Bart doesn't get along well with Lisa. My theory is that they

> ### *I Do Data*
>
> According to the Association of Bridal Consultants, couples tend to follow these trends in selecting attendants:
>
> - 93 percent of brides will have a maid of honor.
> - Of bridesmaids, 19 percent of weddings will have two, 19 percent will have three, and 20 percent will have four.
> - 61 percent of weddings will have a flower girl, but only 49 percent of weddings will have a ring bearer.
> - 97 percent of grooms choose a best man.
> - Of ushers, 16 percent of weddings will have two, 18 percent will have three, and 18 percent will have four.

were married in a previous life, in a *War of the Roses* type of deal, and they killed each other, only to be reunited through me in this life," she says, only half-jokingly. While Tina didn't want to cave in to Bart's demands completely, she didn't want to ignore his feelings either. Their compromise? Instead of having Lisa be in the wedding per se, Tina asked Lisa to do a reading during the ceremony. So that Lisa would feel special, Tina ordered a corsage for her to wear and thanked her in the program. "It worked out very nicely," Tina adds.

Learning to compromise is not only crucial in choosing attendants but in marriage itself. "What you need to prepare for a marriage is the opportunity to negotiate, to compromise, and to work through what is needed for this wedding to succeed," says Beatty. So, in essence, planning a wedding is like a rehearsal of your married life. If the two of you can figure out a way to make your wedding be the way you both want it to be—attendants included—and come away without feeling like you sacrificed something, then chances are you'll have a great marriage.

Who Can Afford to Be an Attendant?

The other criteria I suggest using in picking attendants is based on finances, availability, and other life circumstances that may affect a person's ability to be involved in your wedding.

For example, if one of your friends is going to be visibly pregnant by the time you walk down the aisle, you'll probably want to let her know that you'd really like her to be in your wedding, but you will understand if she declines. When she's nine-months pregnant, she probably won't want to have to waddle down the aisle in an aubergine dress that makes her feel like Moby Dick. You should probably make the same no-strings-attached offer to any friend who has young children. The key, though, isn't to exclude them without an explanation but to make them the offer they can refuse—that is, ask them to be in the wedding but explain that you'll understand if they need to decline because of _____ (pregnancy/small children/unresolved issues with dyeable shoes—you fill in the blank). One bride I know told two of her girlfriends, both graduate students, that she decided not to ask them to be bridesmaids because she figured they couldn't afford it on graduate student salaries. Of course, her friends were crushed—not because they were embarrassed about not having a lot of money (both said they would have taken out loans or started working nights at a strip club to afford it), but because their friend had gone ahead and made the decision for them. "By the time they told me that they could afford to be in my wedding, it was too late to include them," she told me. "I felt just awful about it."

Volunteers Not Wanted

What if the opposite happens? People you hadn't considered—or desperately despise—ask to be in your wedding or, even worse, volunteer. This is what happened to Rose in Miami. "Some friends volunteered themselves as bridesmaids as soon as my fiancé and I announced our engagement," she recalls. "This put me in an awkward position because they weren't the people I would ask to be my bridesmaids." Not only did these friends volunteer, but they began to actively lobby for the bridesmaids' positions. "Every time we spoke on the phone, they would bring it up. I just changed the subject," says Rose, who altogether stopped talking to these over-eager bridesmaid wannabes.

While Rose's plan will work for the short term, the best way to handle the bridesmaid volunteer corps problem is to nip it in the bud. Don't laugh in their faces or say something like, "You're kidding, right?" Instead, the Cohans suggest that you say to the person something to the effect of "I'm very touched that you want to be a bridesmaid, and I'll take you into consideration when I make my decision. However, I'm not ready to make that decision yet, and I thank you for offering." Don't feel guilty about excluding someone, because lying to them and to yourself will just create a recipe for disaster.

If one of the volunteers is someone you'd like to be a part of your wedding, just not in your bridal party, there are a number of ways to include him or her in the wedding. Here's a list of suggestions:

- One person can manage the guest book. This job is great for someone who is outgoing and won't be shy about approaching guests to sign the book.

- Another person can do a reading or sing a song during the ceremony. Obviously, you'll want to choose someone who isn't afraid of speaking in public or who doesn't sound like a frog when he or she sings. (Experience in a church choir is probably a good prerequisite here.)

- Someone can hand out programs at the ceremony.

- Some people can act as ushers. Sure, most ushers are guys, but if you have an overwhelming number of female friends you want to involve—and you don't mind shaking up tradition a little bit—have some of your girlfriends escort people to their seats.

- Other people can distribute rice or birdseed for guests to throw as you leave the church, synagogue, or wherever it is you're going to tie the knot.

No matter what you decide to assign your friends to do, make sure you list them in your program and, if possible, order a corsage or boutonniere for them to wear. That way they'll stand out in the crowd and it will help them feel as if they are a special part of your special day, which they are.

One bride I know took the corsage idea one step further. She wanted her friends doing readings and such, those who couldn't actually be bridesmaids, to feel as if they were. So she asked those friends to come dressed in an outfit of their own that was the same color as the bridesmaid dresses so when they all had pictures taken together, it would look like they were in the wedding party. What a beautiful gesture.

Dressing Your Attendants

If there's one stereotype that continues to persist throughout weddings it is the awful bridesmaid dresses that a woman chooses for her friends to wear. Thankfully, bridesmaid dress designers have finally embraced high fashion, and no longer do bridesmaids need to wear fuschia froufrou frocks—that is, unless the bride wants them to. This is your day and you can choose to dress your bridesmaids in any way you see fit. But before you send your girlfriends off to try on something that looks like the prom dress from hell, consider some of the trends in bridesmaid wear.

The truth is more and more brides are becoming very hands *off* when it comes to bridesmaid dresses. "Either the bride picks three or four dresses that she likes and then lets each bridesmaid choose dresses from that selection, or she'll choose a manufacturer and a fabric and let the bridesmaids choose a dress that fits her criteria," says Daphne Silverstein, owner of The Bridal Party, a by-appointment-only shop in New York City that sells just bridesmaid dresses. The great thing about choosing dresses in the same color is you get a cohesive look for your photo-

❧ Doing It Her Way ❧

"I have five bridesmaids. Two of them are smaller than size 2, two are tall, and one will be nine months pregnant by the time of my wedding. Given the diverse shapes and sizes, finding dresses was going to prove challenging.

"One day we'd all gone shopping to look for dresses, and we found ourselves at designer Cynthia Rowley's shop in Soho. We found a handful of fun dresses all made from the same fabric—a black organza with embroidered pastel-colored flowers.

"Everyone tried on the dresses, and my attendants ended up choosing three styles of dresses made with that fabric—a spaghetti-strap dress, a dress with an A-line skirt, and a 1950s-style party dress. Even though these are three very different looking dresses, the fabric is idiosyncratic enough that it will tie the different styles together."

—Leonore, New York City

graphs. If you let each bridesmaid choose her own style dress, she can find something that flatters her figure. Adds Silverstein, "You should always consider the body types of your bridesmaids. If you've got size 2 and size 22 bridesmaids, I think they should be wearing different dresses."

Having her bridesmaids feel good about the dresses they would wear at her wedding was a top priority for Julia of Princeton, New Jersey. "I wanted my bridesmaids to feel comfortable and attractive and not feel pressured to buy an ugly and expensive dress that they would never wear again," says Julia, who simply told them to find burgundy dresses they liked and would want to wear to the wedding. "One bridesmaid bought a dress that suited her tastes, and the other bridesmaid already had a dress that was the perfect color. It worked out wonderfully."

While things worked out well for Julia, I wouldn't suggest giving your bridesmaids a lot of freedom with the dresses. If you want a pulled-together look, then you'll need to be specific about colors and fabric types. Getting a swatch of fabric for them to use may be the best way to handle the situation.

Another great way to pull off an original look with your bridesmaids is to encourage them to buy separates. The newest trend in bridesmaid

➤✤ *Doing It Her Way* ✤➤

Marisa, a New York City bride, had looked in a handful of bridesmaid stores as well as Bloomingdale's in search of her ideal bridesmaid dress. "I had a vision of something out of Jane Austen's *Emma*, with people walking across a field in flowing dresses, and something in satin chartreuse just wouldn't cut it," says Marisa. None of the shops she visited had anything that fit her vision—until she checked out Daffy's, a discount clothing shop. "I walked into Daffy's one day during my lunch break, and as I was flipping through the racks, I found this light mustard yellow sun dress," Marisa recalls. Not only was the dress flowing (perfect for walking through a field of flowers), but it came in sizes to fit all her bridesmaids and was marked down from $300 to $89. Marisa bought the dresses and her ideal vision of her wedding came true when her friends walked down the aisle in those dresses from Daffy's.

wear isn't dresses but skirts and tops (a.k.a. separates) in a variety of fabrics and colors that can be mixed and matched. The skirts come in A-line, pleated, short, and long. The tops come in all sleeve lengths (including sleeveless). Fabric choices include velvet, satin, and organza. In keeping with the separates look, Silverstein of The Bridal Party likes to encourage brides to have their attendants buy one of the skirts and then go to their favorite store to buy a matching twinset. (Imagine, picking up a sweater twinset at Target or Talbots to wear in a wedding party. That's so cool!) "With twinsets being so important in regular fashion markets, using them as part of a bridesmaid ensemble makes it easy for people to pull together their own looks," says Silverstein.

No matter how you decide to dress your bridesmaids, keep the following tips in mind:

• Hold off deciding what you want your bridesmaids to wear until you've actually chosen your bridal party. That's because the number of attendants you have may determine where you go shopping. If you just need to dress a few girls, you may be able to pick something up off the rack. A larger bridal party, on the other hand, may fare better by getting custom-made dresses.

• Speaking of larger, if you decide to dress your bridesmaids alike, make sure the dress you choose is the one that flatters your zaftig bridesmaid first. Skinny girls look good in anything, but the same can't be said for plus-size bridesmaids, so be sensitive to their needs.

• Try really hard to find a dress that costs less than a car payment. It may seem reasonable for you, the bride, to spend a lot of money on your dress. You can save your dress and pass it down to your daughter someday. But

⊸ Doing It Her Way ⊱

"Each of my bridesmaids is a different size and height. They range from five feet four inches to six feet tall. I knew that having one style of dress for all four girls would never work. Since I'd hired someone to create a wedding dress based on sketches of what I wanted, I asked her to make dresses for my bridesmaids, too. They worked with the seamstress to create individual gowns that flattered each girl's figure.

"To tie the look of the different styles of dresses together, I had the seamstress use the same color (navy blue) and fabrics (chiffon and satin). Then I had the bridesmaids wear the same pearl-and-silver earrings and silver shoes.

"They were so beautiful, and I loved seeing their personalities shine through. It was the right decision not to try and make them all look uniform. They loved the freedom to be themselves, and it showed in how relaxed they were."

—*Tracey, Burlington, Massachusetts*

I've yet to hear of a bridesmaid who so loved her bridesmaid dress that she looked forward to wearing it again or making it a family heirloom.

• Get over the idea of finding a dress that your bridesmaids will wear again. While you may think the dress is flattering enough for someone to wear to an office party or another formal event, your bridesmaids may have differing opinions.

• If you can, help your bridesmaids pay for their dresses, if not buy them yourself altogether. Of course, you should ignore my advice to pick up the dress tab if the dress you've chosen is $400 and you're having eight bridesmaids. However, if you look for bargains whenever you can (see Chapter 3, "Doing Your Wedding for Free (Almost)," for some ideas) and are able to find great dresses that don't cost a lot, you can make the grand gesture of paying for your attendants' dresses.

That's what Dina of Westfield, New Jersey did after attending a Vera Wang sample sale. While Dina was there to get her wedding gown, she couldn't resist buying the sage green Vera Wang bridesmaid dresses she stumbled upon. The color was perfect, and the price was definitely right: $50 a pop. "We later saw the same dress at a retail store for $350," says Dina, whose purchases of the dresses were gifts for her three attendants.

⚜ Doing It Her Way ⚜

"I happened to step into a Laura Ashley store one day, thinking they might have a nice dress for my flower girl to wear. As soon as I walked in, I saw some pretty pale-pink dresses that I thought would be perfect for my bridesmaids. There were only two left, and they were in the sizes I needed. To top it all off, they were 50 percent off! I got them for $75 each. I decided for two reasons to pair the dresses with pink cardigans. One, I got married in March, and it's hard to tell what the weather would be like. And, two, I think the cardigans look great with the dresses and really pulled the whole look together."

—*Caroline, St. Louis, Missouri*

Your Way or No Way

You thought finding the right guy to marry was one of the hardest decisions you'd have to make in your adult life. Well, figuring out who should be in your bridal party is right up there with major life decisions. While experts say that true friends will understand if you don't choose them to be in your wedding, reality bites. Friends will get upset if you don't include them and so you have to approach the choice of attendants decision with caution. Here are some things to keep in mind:

- ❦ Choose friends with whom you've shared major life events. A friend who has stuck by you through the tough times will be there when you need her at your wedding.

- ❦ Don't ask anyone before consulting your fiancé first. Each person you have in your wedding party should be someone you both like (at least a little bit) and agree is the best man or woman for the job.

- ❦ If you have to exclude people, involve them in your wedding somehow. Give them a reading to do during the ceremony or ask them to man the guest book.

- ❦ Be sensitive to your attendants' needs when choosing attire, including the price of the garb and what it looks like.

3

DOING YOUR WEDDING FOR FREE (ALMOST)

I recently read a study that said one of the ways that the rich stay rich is by taking advantage of bargains. They don't simply shop at places like Marshall's or TJ Maxx or clip coupons at the supermarket. What sets rich people's bargain-hunting ability apart from the masses' is the fact that when something is really cheap, the rich can buy a lot of it because they've got cash to spare. They can get away without paying full price for many things, if they think ahead and shop when the sales are good—not when they need something. The rest of us usually can only afford to go shopping when we've allocated a little extra money for a shopping splurge, which, unfortunately, may not be when the best sales are.

I have honed my bargain-hunting abilities over the years and, thanks to wise investing by my husband, we have enough of a savings portfolio that I now have the freedom to snap up large quantities of discount items whenever I stumble upon a really good sale. For example, I was visiting a bookstore in early February and noticed that they still had leftover Christmas merchandise on sale. When I went to the sale table, I couldn't believe what I saw: boxes of high-quality Christmas cards (twenty cards and envelopes per box, originally priced at $13.50 per box) and rolls of wrapping paper (originally $5) both for $1 each. I cleaned the place out and spent only $12. Now, when Christmas rolls around, I won't have to spend my snowy afternoons fighting the madding holiday crowds — or paying inflated prices. (Who's ever heard of coming away from the stores during the holiday rush and spending only $12?)

Ask any money-saving expert about the clever ways to stretch your dollar, and he/she'll tell you that the key to real bargain shopping is stocking up on things when they are on sale. You may find that you won't touch these items for a few weeks or months, but when you eventually need them, you'll already own them and you won't have to pay full price. Let me give you another personal example.

At the end of last summer, the Disney store was having a huge sale. (I've got two kids, so I'm in the Disney store a lot. Wait a few years and you'll be shopping there, too.) Bathing suits featuring popular Disney characters were marked down from $20 to $5. With two growing kids who are big Disney fans, I knew these bathing suits would be a valuable commodity come summer time — or Disney vacation, like the one we were planning for the following January. I snapped up bathing suits in my daughters' sizes — and the sizes they would be growing into during the next few years. For $30, I got three years' worth of bathing suits, and my kids were thrilled when we arrived at Disney World and they had Minnie Mouse and Princess Jasmine bathing suits to wear to the pool.

Now if you like a good bargain like I do and you know how to be a smart shopper, you may worry that you'll have to throw away all your good shopping sense when it comes time to plan your wedding. Not true; there are a lot of creative ways to do your wedding for practically free, especially if you're into making things yourself or willing to invest a little time to go that extra mall lap to find a good price.

For example, the next time you go to a stationery store, crafts store, mass merchandiser, or office-supply superstore, check out the sales. Are there any items on sale that you might be able to work into your wedding to replace something more expensive? For example, if you're planning on going the traditional route of wrapping almonds in tulle and giving them away as favors, maybe you can find a less expensive and more tasty option on sale after major candy holidays, such as Halloween, Christmas, Valentine's Day, or Easter. See what kinds of pastel-colored candy is left over after Easter, for example. You may find that you can put together clusters of pretty-hued candy favors for just pennies apiece.

Or if you'd like to do something with a love theme, start haunting the stores the day after Valentine's Day, when retailers will surely want to get rid of everything red and shaped like a heart. Look for marked-down heart-shaped bowls that you can use as centerpieces at your reception or heart-shaped frames to give as gifts to your attendants. Remember: you may not be thinking about centerpieces or attendants' gifts in February, but if you're planning on using hearts anywhere in your wedding, you'll find the best sales on everything hearts right after Valentine's Day. Think about it this way: if you want something heart-shaped for your wedding and you hit the stores looking for it in September, either you won't be able to find anything anywhere (retailers probably stock hearts only in

February), or if you do find something you like, you'll have to pay an exorbitant price for it.

There really are hundreds of ways to be a bargain-savvy shopper and a creative cost-cutter when planning your wedding. Read on for some wonderful ways to save money on your wedding without skimping on quality.

General Advice

- If you live in a big city but grew up somewhere else (where the cost of living is less), have your wedding there. One Chicago bride I know decided that having her wedding in her fiancé's hometown in Iowa made much more sense than trying to throw together a less-than-dreamed about wedding in the Windy City. For the amount of money she would have spent on just the flowers in Chicago, she paid for her entire wedding in Iowa.

- Move your wedding to a less popular day of the week or time of day. Maria and John in Alexandria, Virginia, wanted a hotel wedding but didn't want to pay downtown Washington, D.C., prices. So they booked a nearby airport hotel and moved their wedding up a few hours—from a Saturday night dinner affair to a Saturday afternoon luncheon. Thanks to the location and time move together, Maria and John were able to save $25 per person on reception costs.

- If you've got a special talent, see if you can barter it for a discount or, even better, for free services for your wedding. Lisa, a writer in upstate

New York, convinced a local limousine company to let her write some marketing materials for them in exchange for transportation at her wedding.

Here's another example of creative bartering: "I know a bride, a dog breeder, who gave away a puppy in exchange for her wedding cake," says Sharon Naylor, author of *1,001 Ways to Save Money and Still Have a Dazzling Wedding* (Contemporary Books, 1994). Naylor says she's also heard of accountant grooms doing a vendor's taxes in exchange for a service at their wedding.

Here's a clincher: one savvy bride, a travel writer who always dreamed of getting married on a tropical isle, pitched her idea to a variety of vendors on a certain Caribbean isle. They, in turn, promised to plan her wedding for free if she were to write about them in a story. Once she landed an assignment with a magazine (the magazine knew about her quid pro quo arrangement), she and her fiancé were off to a free wed-

---

~☙ NEWS YOU CAN USE: OFF-PEAK WEDDINGS ❧~

If you're looking to save money or stand out from the crowd by having your wedding at an offbeat time, consider the following statistics from the Association of Bridal Consultants:

- Only 10 percent of weddings take place on Sundays, and only 12 percent occur in the morning.
- 7 percent of weddings take place in gardens or other outside places.
- January, February, and March are the least popular months in which to have a wedding.

ding in paradise. The only catch: she didn't have any input into anything that happened at the wedding, and she couldn't bring any guests. But she and her groom had a great time anyway.

• Know how to use a computer? Then use it to make everything and anything printed for your wedding—invitations, programs, menus, and place cards for the reception. Catalogs like Paper Direct and office-supply stores sell card stock and software specifically designed to help do-it-yourselfers make their own wedding invitations for a fraction of the price of hiring a stationer. Another great tip: find a calligraphy-like font on your computer for addressing your envelopes. Sure, it won't be hand-done calligraphy, but unless you're inviting Ms. Wedding Etiquette to your nuptials, who cares?

❧ Doing It Her Way ❧

"We are sending a postcard as a response card instead of a card plus envelope. This saves us on invitations' costs and postage, too, since we can buy postcard-rate stamps instead of letter-rate stamps."

—Jeannine, Hoboken, New Jersey

"Someone tipped me off to the fact that you can make your own place cards using a laser printer. You simply buy precut sheets of blank business cards and set up a template on your computer to print your guests' names on the cards." —Dana, New York City

- Want to be a June bride? *Fuggedaboutit.* Because you and everyone else you know wants to tie the knot in June, it is the most popular month for weddings. Instead, try to plan your wedding for when everyone else won't be banging down the vendors' doors. Figure out what peak season is where you live and then plan to have your wedding off-peak. Not only will you have less competition for vendors' services, but you'll probably get price breaks as well.

- If you live in or near a state where clothing is tax-free, go there to buy your wedding attire. For example, many New Yorkers know that if they simply cross the Hudson River into New Jersey, they won't have to pay sales tax on clothing. In fact, a small cottage industry of wedding vendors has cropped up in Fort Lee, New Jersey, just over the George Washington Bridge from Manhattan, probably to attract shoppers looking to save money on clothing purchases.

- See if you can find a place where you can have your wedding for free—or close to it. Many parks and public spaces are available, free of charge, to residents of the town where they are located, or they are available for a small fee. In addition, local civic organizations may own space that they'll rent for a nominal fee, such as $50 to cover cleaning up. For example, a bride I know found out that the local Kiwanis club's headquarters, housed in a huge historic home, was available for rent. The price tag? Seventy-five dollars, which the organization asked simply for maintenance. Being the cheapskate that she is, she negotiated the fee down to nothing by promising that her friends would stay after the party was over and clean up themselves. They did, and she got her reception location for absolutely no charge at all.

• Find out who you know that works in the wedding business and get a quote from him or her. You'll probably find that having a friend in the business will benefit your bottom line. One bride who works in advertising and therefore deals with printers a lot found out that one of her vendors would print her invitations for her at below cost. The final bill? One hundred dollars for 300 invitations. Another bride's uncle worked at a tuxedo rental store and got her groom and his party 50 percent off their entire rental bill. Yet another bride knew someone who worked in New York's diamond district, and she was able to get her engagement ring for the wholesale price. Other brides and grooms have told me about the wedding guest who donated his or her talent as a gratis to benefit the couple at their wedding, like the deejay who spun tunes at the reception and held onto the $900 bill he normally charges couples for his services. I'm not saying you should ask your friends outright to do something for free at your wedding, but if someone offers, take him or her up on it.

1 Do Data

According to the Association of Bridal Consultants, the wedding market generates as much as $38 billion annually.

Ceremony

• Book a college chapel if you can; you'll get a discount if you're an alumni or are related to someone who is. When Bill and I were planning our original wedding, we booked the chapel at a college on Long Island that has a beautiful multidenominational chapel on a hill overlooking the bucolic campus. Because Bill's dad had graduated from this school, the college would charge only a few hundred dollars to rent the chapel.

~❧ *Doing It Her Way* ❧~

"Since my parents were flying in from out of state and had to rent a car anyway, I decided to forgo a limousine and, instead, asked my dad if he could rent a nice white car as a 'gift.' He was more than happy to have an excuse to rent a big, roomy car. The white Lincoln Town Car looked just as nice as a limo, was easier to park in our crowded little town, and having Dad as the chauffeur was considerably more reliable than the limo driver from hell I'd heard about who stranded a bride on the New Jersey Turnpike." —*Mary, Lambertville, New Jersey*

Jeannine and Todd of Hoboken, New Jersey, got a great deal from their alma mater when they booked the college chapel for their ceremony. "The chapel is normally $150 to rent, but because we're alumni, we got it for half price: $75!" says Jeannine.

• Does your church or synagogue have a great choir? Ask them to perform at your ceremony. Many times, they'll do it for free.

• To save on decorations, pick a ceremony site that is naturally beautiful or comes with its own decorations. The great thing about Christmas weddings, for instance, is most churches are already festively decorated for the holidays so you don't have to bring in your own flowers. Getting married in

I Do Data

Of winter weddings, 11 percent are Christmas weddings, according to the Society of American Florists.

a botanical garden? Great. You've just saved yourself the need to hire a florist for your ceremony.

• Consider using dried flowers instead of fresh. The cost for one bouquet of dried flowers is about the same as a Starbucks coffee, which is considerably less than what fresh-cut flowers cost.

• Don't worry about hiring a videographer to tape the ceremony, if you don't want a fancy finished videotape anyway. Instead, set up a videocamera where it can film the entire ceremony from one location and have the tape rolling throughout the ceremony.

• Are you having a short ceremony? Why not avoid the cost of renting chairs and have your guests stand around you as you exchange vows? It's a great way to make the setting more intimate.

• Remember the three Rs: reuse, reuse, reuse. There's nothing shameful about reusing someone's wedding decorations at your ceremony, as long as they are in good condition, of course. So find out if your church or synagogue is having a ceremony before yours, and then see if they'll allow you to reuse the flowers—assuming the previous bride won't be needing them anymore. Another great way to reuse is to take the decorations from the church along with you to the reception.

Rehearsal Dinner

• If you're having your wedding in a hotel, inn, or bed-and-breakfast— and your guests are staying there, too—use those facilities for your rehearsal dinner as well. For example, a bed-and-breakfast may require

~≪ *Doing It Her Way* ≫~

"We got married on a Sunday afternoon. The affair that would take place the night before was going to have a beautiful *huppah*—a Jewish wedding canopy—provided by the florist who I happened to be using as well. The synagogue was also going to be fully decorated with flowers that the bride was not going to take with her to the reception. My florist happened to tell me this during a casual conversation, so I asked him if there was any way we could use the *huppah* and keep the flowers for my wedding the next day. He checked with the other bride, and she said it was fine. By asking him, I saved $2,000 on decorations. And the flowers stayed fresh and still looked fine the next day." —*Joanna, Westchester, New York*

a two nights' stay at minimum, so all of your guests will already be around the night before your wedding. To save time, effort, and, most important, money on your rehearsal dinner, have it at the bed-and-breakfast, too. If you've booked a number of your guests at the hotel where your wedding will be, see what kind of discount you can get the hotel to give you. For one couple, the hotel offered them 20 percent off on their rehearsal dinner.

• Have your rehearsal dinner at a place where something else is going on, like a local carnival or a bowling alley. Not only will it be more fun for those involved, but you won't have to pay extra for the entertainment: it will already be there.

Reception

• When in doubt, make your centerpieces yourself. Lorelei, a bride in Ann Arbor, Michigan, made table-sized topiaries (supplies from Frank's), which cost her only $80. An even cheaper option is what southern Californians Carmen and Malcolm did. They knew their wedding guests were primarily chocaholics, so their centerpieces were quite tasty. They invested in glass bowls ($1 each) and filled them with gold and silver Hershey's kisses. Total cost? About $30. "People could snack on them and they looked pretty," recalls Carmen.

• Don't spend money on a band or a deejay if your guests don't intend to dance. Instead, take your CD player, insert your favorite—and party-appropriate—CDs, and voilà! You've got four hours of great music for no cost whatsoever.

• Stock your own bar but limit the selections. Red and white wine, champagne, and sodas should be just fine. Even better, buy from a liquor store that will allow you to return unopened bottles for a refund.

• If your friends won't think you rude for asking, have a potluck wedding reception. Carmen and Malcolm, mentioned above, happened to be planning their wedding right after a California earthquake. "We simply couldn't afford a caterer," recalls Carmen. So they asked a handful of their friends if they would each bring a covered dish that would feed twenty people to the wedding, and their friends obliged. At Carmen and Malcolm's wedding, guests dined on homemade tamales, Mexican rice, pasta salad, and chocolate-chip cookies.

Attire

• Whether you're buying bridesmaids' dresses or renting tuxedos, if you're giving one store a lot of business, ask for a volume discount.

• Afraid of ruining your $7 pantyhose on your wedding day? Invest in a $.99 bottle of clear nail polish so you can stop any runs before they get out of control. Better yet, forget the expensive pantyhose and stock up on stockings when they're on sale at your local drugstore. No one will know whether you're wearing L'Eggs or Donna Karan hose at your wedding anyway, so why not save yourself some money and go with the cheaper pantyhose? That way if your husband puts his finger through

⇝ *Doing It Her Way* ⇜

"I purchased my wedding gown in a rather unique way—I saw a classified ad for it in the newspaper. At the time, we were living in Chicago and trying to do the wedding on a tight budget. The dress was in my size, and I called on a whim.

"I went to this woman's house to see it—I actually tried it on in her living room—and absolutely loved it. It was a mermaid style, with sheer long sleeves and beading all over. The best part? It cost only $150. I got a ton of compliments on the dress at the wedding, and I've yet to reveal my secret." —*Melanie, Dallas, Texas*

your stockings as he's taking off the garter, you can run to the bathroom afterward, switch pantyhose, and only lose a couple dollars instead of ten.

• Find out if the dress designer you like has a location at an outlet mall near you. One bride had her heart set on a Jessica McClintock dress and discovered that she could find wedding-quality dresses (but not necessarily wedding dresses) at the local Jessica McClintock outlet. Instead of spending $1,500 for something that was labeled a wedding dress, she was able to pick up a gown (probably intended for a prom) for only $300.

• Speaking of proms, check out the sales racks after prom season has come and gone. Many dresses that high school students wear to their prom can double as bridesmaids' dresses. And once the proms are over, stores will be looking to move the merchandise, so you should find some great sales.

• If you live in a show-business city, see if there are any costume shops where you can rent a wedding dress. Who knows? Someone famous may have worn the very same dress in a movie.

• Consider having your gown made, especially if you know a good seamstress who will do the job for practically nothing.

• Wear your mom's, sister's, or aunt's gown if it's in good condition, it fits you, and you like it. There's no better way to save money on clothing than to accept hand-me-downs. Plus the sentimental quality of wearing a close relative's or friend's dress at your wedding is priceless.

Photography

• Hire a photographer who shoots a lot of parties but not necessarily weddings. This is a great option for those who work in an industry where party planning (and attending) is part of the job, such as advertising, public relations, and publishing. See if your event-planning department has a photographer they can recommend. He or she will probably only charge an hourly rate and won't make you buy an expensive photo album to boot.

• If you really don't care about professional-looking photographs at the reception, invest in disposable cameras and give them out to all your guests so they can become your wedding photographers. So you won't miss out on formal portraits, arrange to have pictures taken with a professional photographer on a separate date after the wedding. It will be a lot cheaper than hiring him or her to cover your entire wedding.

❧ NEWS YOU CAN USE: SEW YOUR OWN ❧

The Home Sewing Association, a trade organization, offers a website (www.sewing.org) with instructions and advice on how to make your own wedding gown. The only thing the site doesn't offer is actual patterns. You'll have to go to your local fabric shop to pick one up. If you're interested in other wedding-related sewing projects, this website also offers tips on how to sew attendants' clothes, make goodie bags for guests, or create a money bag for holding wedding envelopes.

Your Way or No Way

There are a number of ways to do your wedding for almost free, and many of them involve you, your fiancé, and your friends using a little elbow grease to make things yourselves. What's great about putting in the extra effort to make centerpieces or do your own invitations is it adds your own unique touch to your wedding. Keep the following in mind when looking for ways to save money on your wedding plans:

- Move the time or date of your wedding to off-peak, so to speak, when vendors will be less in demand and prices will be cheaper.

- Make much of your wedding paraphernalia yourself if doing so actually saves you money. However, if you want to make your own gown but you don't know how to sew, the time it will take for you to learn this skill plus the money you'll invest for the dress fabric will probably have a higher price tag, when you consider the hassle factor, than if you'd purchased your dress the standard way.

- Hire anyone you know personally (and respect) in the wedding business to be involved in your wedding. You'll probably net yourself a sweet discount or your friend might even throw in his or her services for free as a gift.

- Always be on the lookout for sales on things you'll need at your wedding, be it candy for favors, napkins for your rehearsal dinner, or pantyhose for you and your bridesmaids.

- Reuse everything. Find out if the church or temple where you're going to be married is having a wedding before yours. Ask whether the decorations that bride will be using will remain—and whether you could use them, too. Or, if you use your own decorations for the ceremony, take them with you to the reception and have them double as centerpieces on the tables. For example, if you decorate the pews with small clusters of flowers, those could easily double as tabletop decorations. Finally, if a friend or relative has offered her wedding gown, take her up on her offer. Of course, don't just do this for money-saving's sake. If you're close to this person, you like her dress, and it fits you well or only needs minor alterations, wearing it will save a ton of money on your attire and add the something borrowed to the list of traditions many brides like to follow at their weddings.

❧ 4 ❧

GIFTS: REGISTERING, RECEIVING, AND GIVING

A wedding is a big gift-giving event. There are the gifts you give to your attendants and also to each other; this chapter will help you figure out the best presents for those situations. Of course, the most top-of-mind gifts when it comes to weddings are those that your guests will give to you. The bridal registry is of paramount importance to the process of giving and receiving wedding gifts. No hard-and-fast rule says you must register for your wedding gifts, but it is almost assumed these days. Having gone through a wedding without registering, let me tell you that you'll make your life a lot easier—as well as the lives of your guests—if you drop your qualms and register.

One of the reasons Bill and I didn't register was the whole idea made him uncomfortable. He didn't like telling people what to buy us as wedding gifts, and he didn't want to take the time to select gifts. Also the fact that we'd lived both on our own and together for many years meant that,

---

⫷ Doing It Their Way ⫸

"We didn't register for gifts, and we didn't ask our guests to give us gifts either. Instead, we suggested that people send donations to our two favorite charities." —*Terry and Mike, Raleigh, North Carolina*

---

frankly, we didn't need the traditional housewares usually associated with registering. (If only Home Depot had had its registry program up and running when we got married in 1992. Then registering would have been a nonissue, and Bill would have been dragging *me* to the store to register.) Put both of those reasons together, and you have a couple not registering.

But it's not that simple. We soon found out that our decision not to register didn't make our life easier. In fact, it made it more difficult. Because wedding guests assume that couples have at least registered for china, crystal, and silver, suddenly our parents were bombarded with phone calls from friends and relatives about our patterns. Our parents didn't know what to do. So they told us, "Get thee to a department store." After work a few nights later, Bill and I went to Macy's. No, we didn't register (we were still determined to buck tradition), but we did at least pick china and stemware patterns we could live with. In retrospect, we should have registered then and there, because, in essence, we ended up registering with our mothers! That is, our mothers were each given a list of the patterns and place settings we were interested in receiving. When a guest wanted to buy something or report that he or she had purchased something, that guest had to call one of our mothers to report what had been purchased. Then, to avoid duplicate gifts, whichever mother had received the call had to call the other mother so that she could remove the particular item from the list. It was an awfully tedious process, and I'm sorry we put our mothers through it.

Our nonregistering made life difficult after the wedding, too. There were a number of people who hadn't called our mothers when they bought gifts, and suddenly we were faced with more china and crystal than we knew what to do with. In addition, some people had mistaken the china pattern and given us plates that didn't match anything else we owned. Furthermore, returns were difficult to accomplish because we hadn't established a relationship with a store through its gift registry. Our mantra after the wedding became "If only we'd registered. If only."

Registering for Gifts

So, even if it's against your better judgment, register. Lucky for you you're getting married in a time when stuffy department stores that stock expensive china and crystal aren't your only option for registering. Just as you can personalize your honeymoon or your ceremony, the same can be done for registering.

If you're big on sports, you can register at places like L.L. Bean, REI, or Campmor. I've heard of couples who happened to be buying or renovating a home around the time of their wedding, and registering at a

I Do Data

The Association of Bridal Consultants says that the bridal market accounts for the purchase of 29 percent of all living room furniture, 31 percent of all bedroom furniture, 22 percent of linen and bedding, 45 percent of glassware, and 33 percent of electronics.

home improvement store (Home Depot, Lowe's Home Improvement Warehouse, you name it) made the most sense. They added to their list practical things they would need on a day-to-day basis, such as screw drivers, smoke alarms, and snow shovels. "Some people register for projects," says Katrina Blauvelt, a spokesperson for Home Depot, which offers a computerized registry system available in all of its stores nationwide. "You can register for a new kitchen, and guests can put funds toward the project or they can actually buy your new cabinets for you." The attraction of registering in a home improvement store is so widespread that it draws in celebrities as well as regular folk. "Our most famous registrants were [actors] Ted Danson and Mary Steenburgen," says Blauvelt. Guys who wish they were Tim "The Tool Man" Taylor will love knowing that Sears finally offers a registry program, and there's one area of the registry devoted specifically to Craftsmen tools.

Another way to personalize your registry is to register at a store where you love to shop. Callie and Mike of Hoboken, New Jersey, love shopping at Target, so when they got engaged, they decided that Target would

---

✷ Doing It Their Way ✷

"We chose to register at Target because of the quality merchandise, low prices, and great selections. Because we didn't need traditional stuff, we registered for movies, lamp shades, picture frames, video games, and a toolbox. Nobody had anything negative to say about their experience at Target. Plus, it was really fun to go around the store scanning things."

—*Shelly and Eddie, Dallas, Texas*

be one of the stores where they registered their preferences. The process of registering was easy and fun.

On the day Callie and Mike went to register, they signed in at the Club Wedd kiosk, which is located at the front of each Target store. After entering their basic information (name, wedding date, etc.), they printed out their registration form and took it to the customer service desk, at which time they were given a scanner gun to record their gift selections. After circling the store a couple of times and finishing their scanning, they returned the scanner to customer service, where the information from the scanner was downloaded into Target's computer system. Within minutes, Callie and Mike's gift list was available for all guests to access at any Target store.

What's great about registering at a place like Target is you can ask for the basic everyday stuff along with funkier stuff. "We've registered for a toaster oven, a coffeemaker, kitchen towels, a chenille throw, suitcases, a bread maker, and cookie sheets. We've also registered for a Sony Playstation, a television, a VCR, and a few board games," says Callie, who is happy to report that she received the Sony Playstation as a holiday gift from her father. "At my bridal shower, the Target items were by far the most popular. People really seem to enjoy having an alternative to the normal registry items, and we've received a lot of cool gifts that we'll really enjoy having."

Another reason guests like a store such as Target are the prices. "We needed a basic coffeemaker. Mike and I aren't big coffee drinkers, but we wanted to have one for when we have guests," Callie recalls. "At one of the other stores where we registered for high-end dishes, they had beautiful coffeemakers, but they were $80. At Target, we were able to get a $20 coffeemaker that was more suited to our needs."

Please understand that I'm not a paid spokesperson for Target. But, having become a bona fide gift-giving expert over time, I can honestly say that I believe Target offers one of the best registries out there.

If you'd like to track down interesting and unusual places to register, check out my first book, *The Bridal Registry Book*, which lists more than one hundred places to register, many of which you never knew existed. Another great way to find places to register—and to actually register your gift preferences—is via the Internet. For example, America Online recently announced "Weddings@AOL," which includes links to various bridal registries, including Macy's On-line (www.macys.com) and The Wedding Network (www.weddingnetwork.com), which offers its own links to retailers in twenty-six categories. Those retailers range from beer to books, sporting goods to gourmet food. What's cool about registering on-line is you can do it when it's convenient for you, and not only when the stores are open.

✖ *Doing It Their Way* ✖

"We decided to register exclusively through catalogs. That way we knew that our guests' gifts would arrive quickly and safely, and most of our guests wouldn't have to pay sales tax."

—Karen and Rich, Phoenix, Arizona

Another terrific registry option, especially if you'll have guests coming from all over the country, is to register with a catalog. That way your friends and family won't have to schlepp to a specific store to buy you a gift. Instead, they can call a toll-free number and do everything over the phone. In addition, many catalogs now have websites that allow you to access registry lists and purchase gifts on-line. These options make these registries doubly convenient. That is, your tech-fearful grandmother can buy her gifts using the toll-free number while your tech-savvy best friend will be able to simultaneously surf the Net and buy your gift.

One of the reasons that Houston couple Kelli and Scott chose to register at Ross-Simons, a fairly traditional mail-order company offering china, crystal, and stemware through its catalog and website, was they wanted a place that all their guests could access. "We placed our Waterford crystal and informal Wedgewood patterns on the Ross-Simons registry so that our family and friends around the world would have access to on-line or toll-free ordering and shipment directly to us," says Kelli. Because Ross-Simons (www.ross-simons.com) has retail stores in only six states (Georgia, Maine, Massachusetts, New Jersey, North Carolina, and Rhode Island), guests who live in any of the other forty-four states and buy their gifts from Ross-Simons won't have to pay sales tax on their purchases. The same is true with most other catalog companies. If that company doesn't have business operations in the state where you or your guests live, you won't have to pay what's called use-tax on your purchases. Think about it: if you register with a catalog, not only are you making it easier for your guests to buy gifts, but you're saving them money as well.

Even though Bill and I didn't register, we figured we could at least save our guests money on gifts: we researched which companies had our china in stock and at reasonable prices. And I can tell you from personal experience that Ross-Simons was the one company that had the highest quality of customer service and the most competitive prices—and they always had our china in stock. Most of our guests ended up ordering our gifts from Ross-Simons.

Some of our guests who went to a local department store to buy our gifts had to wait four to six weeks to have their orders processed. What usually happened was they sent us a card telling us that such and such was on order, and when we got the card, we called them, told them to cancel the order with the department store and call Ross-Simons. Our guests were always pleasantly surprised when they called; they discovered that the item was available for immediate delivery and the price was less than what they would have paid at the department store, even with shipping!

Finally, a big trend in registering is registering for your honeymoon. Honeymoon registries usually work in two ways.

First, there are the traditional honeymoon registries, if you can call them that, which allow guests to send money toward a couple's account to help pay for the honeymoon. That money is kept in an escrow account that the couple would eventually use to help pay for their total honeymoon bill. If there was any money left over, they could use it to upgrade their trip or the travel agent would cut them a check for the difference.

This is exactly how Backroads, a company that offers active vacations, runs its registry. You choose which Backroads trip you want to take for your honeymoon (options include biking through France's Loire Valley, hiking in Tuscany, or walking in northern Vermont), put down a $400 deposit, and then notify your guests that they can send contributions to your account. "Each person who sends money toward your account gets a personalized letter acknowledging his or her contribution to your Honeymoon Registry and a gift card that he or she can present to you," says Megan Gaynor, a Backroads spokesperson. "Two weeks prior to the trip's start, we will provide you with a list of all gift givers and their contributions. An invoice will be included, should there be a balance due on the trip."

The second kind of honeymoon registry allows guests to designate which part of the honeymoon they would like to purchase for the couple. With some travel companies, the money the guest sends in is actually used to purchase a specific amenity, such as a massage at a spa at the resort where the couple will be staying. This purchase is arranged through the travel agent who oversees the registry and can book the specific amenity or activity through his or her suppliers. In other instances, the guest's money is earmarked for a certain activity on paper, but in reality it is just used to pay for the honeymoon as a whole. The gift card that the guest receives, however, says that he or she has just purchased such and such activity for the couple to use on the honeymoon.

I Do Data

According to the Association of Bridal Consultants, 26 percent of brides have lived with their fiancé before the wedding. Forty-two percent of married couples will own their own home.

The idea of letting guests buy certain activities on the honeymoon is what attracted Shelly and Eddie of Dallas, Texas, to After I Do Registry (www.afterido.com), also in Dallas. "We had been living together for a long time, so we really didn't need the traditional flatware and stuff, and we love to travel. But we didn't just want to register with a travel agent and have our guests give us cash," says Shelly. "We wanted our friends and relatives to be able to ask, 'How did you like the snorkeling we gave you?' instead of 'Did you get our money?'"

Here are some of the things couples have registered for—and received—through the After I Do Registry:

- lei greeting at Honolulu airport (for a honeymoon in Hawaii, obviously)

- four nights of hotel accommodations

- dinner cruise on a glass-bottomed catamaran

- breakfast in bed

Giving Gifts

With all this talk about registering, it's easy to forget that as bride and groom you aren't only receiving gifts, you will be giving gifts as well—

❦ Doing It Their Way ❦

"After we were pronounced husband and wife, we exchanged a rose. It was our first gift to each other as a married couple. Since a rose means eternal love and faith, it was a most appropriate thing to do. Every year on our anniversary we are going to give each other roses as a way to remember our vows." —*Robyn and Ron, Anaheim, California*

to your attendants, to your family, and to each other. When considering what to give family, attendants, and your future spouse, think about what each person enjoys doing in his or her free time, whether or not he or she has mentioned a particular item of desire, and use both of those pieces of information to help you in your gift buying. For example, if either your dad, your brother, or your husband is a big sports fan and has been lamenting about how he never gets time to attend a baseball/basketball/football game, why not buy each or all of them tickets to a local sporting event?

Or, if your husband has never justified spending money on a good watch and he really should have one (because when he's in a business suit, that free "Rugrats" watch from Burger King just doesn't cut it), then buy him a fancy watch for your wedding gift to him. Likewise, if you think your husband may have a hard time figuring out what to give you for your wedding gift, start dropping hints now. Diamond earrings are always appreciated. Or maybe you're the one wearing the "Rugrats" watch, but you'd really like something a bit more upscale.

1 Do Data

Fifty-six percent of couples give more than ten gifts to their attendants and family members, according to the Association of Bridal Consultants.

When you and your future husband start thinking about what you're going to buy your attendants for gifts, you need to decide whether you're going to purchase them identical gifts or something different for each person. Frankly, the easiest thing to do is to buy everyone identical gifts. While the gesture to buy everyone something different would be nice, the truth is you really don't need the added pressure of buying each of

I Do Data

Gifts account for a small portion of the overall wedding budget. According to the Association of Bridal Consultants, attendants' gifts comprise 1.7 percent of the wedding budget, and gifts the bride and groom give each other comprise only 2.2 percent of the budget.

your attendants a unique gift. Instead, make sure you select something that the largest number of attendants will appreciate.

For example, my husband was a groomsman in a friend's wedding a few years ago. The other groomsmen were either friends from high school or work colleagues of the groom. All of them happened to have a common bond: they loved to fix things. The groom obviously kept this in mind when purchasing the attendants' gifts because he gave each of the men a Leatherman, a fancy version of a Swiss Army knife—with many more gadgets and its own leather pouch, which can clip onto a belt. Each of the groomsmen loved the gift, and my husband still uses his Leatherman whenever he's working on a fix-it project.

Another groom I know is a comedy writer, and all the men in his wedding were involved in humor in one way or another. So what did he get them as gifts? Boxer shorts by Joe Boxer with big smiley faces on them. Everyone loved them.

Following are ten suggested attendant gift ideas:

- Gift certificate for a spa treatment (even *guys* will appreciate this gesture).

- Gift certificate for a favorite store, such as Tower Records or Amazon.com.

- Jewelry that can be worn at the wedding. It's not very original but it is tried and true.

- Jewelry that isn't meant to be worn at the wedding but that the attendants can wear on a regular basis. For girls, that may be pearl earrings or a gold bracelet; for guys, you can get cuff links.

- Souvenirs from the place where you're getting married. Of course, this may border on kitschy, but if you decide to tie the knot in Disney World, wouldn't it be fun to present each of your attendants (and your parents, too) with their own personalized mouse ears?

➤ Doing It Their Way ➤

"There is a custom in Jewish weddings to break a glass at the end of the ceremony, and my friend and I gave each other the same wedding gift: it was a mezuzah made from the glass that our husbands stepped on and broke at our respective ceremonies. There is a company that makes mezuzahs out of clear Lucite and fills them with the pieces of the broken glass from the ceremony. You can pick whatever color glass you want to use, and after your wedding you send it back to the company to have the mezuzah made. We both chose purple glass. You can get more information about this company from places like The Jewish Museum in New York City." —*Michelle, Chicago, Illinois*

"We made our own thank-you notes. We took one of the wedding pictures—a very pretty, candid shot of Tom and me dancing—and had it printed into cards. It wasn't very expensive, and I still see them on friends' and family's refrigerators." —*Sophie and Tom, Dallas, Texas*

⟡ NEWS YOU CAN USE: THANK-YOU NOTES ⟡

While your guests have up to a year after your wedding to send a gift, the reverse is definitely not true when it comes to thank-you notes. In the best of all possible situations (and I realize you're busy people), you should try to have your thank-you note written and sent within eight weeks of your receiving a gift.

The thank-you notes you use can be made to look like your invitations, they can be store-bought, or you can make them yourself. What you don't want to do with thank-you notes, however, is use the kind that come preprinted with a message inside. Okay, you can use them if you want to seriously insult your guests, but that's probably not what you want to do.

Instead, use the blank space inside to convey your sincere appreciation. Make sure you mention the gift specifically in your thank-you note and tell the guest how you're going to use and enjoy it. If you got something you really hate and want to eventually return, please do not share that information with the gift giver. Instead, find one redeeming quality about

- Souvenirs from your wedding. How about having a fun T-shirt made up with you and your future spouse's picture on it and a funny saying that sums up your feelings about having your attendants in your wedding? For example, you could say something like "Sorry if we tied you up in knots as we planned how to tie the knot, but having you in the wedding has meant the world to us."

the gift and talk about it in the thank-you note. Saying something like "The rhinestone-covered statue of Cupid you gave us looks just dazzling in the sunlight" should suffice.

A fun way to add a personal touch to your thank-you notes is to include a photograph of you and your spouse, as many couples do. Why not kick it up a notch by enclosing a picture of you guys with the gift or as you're using the gift? For example, if someone bought you the gas grill you'd registered for, snap a picture of your husband as he's cooking some burgers on it in your backyard. Then send that photo along with the thank-you note to show the gift giver how much you truly appreciate receiving the gift.

You don't have to write a book when you write a thank-you note. Two or three lines of sincere copy will suffice. Besides, if you've got hundreds of thank-you notes to pen, you don't want to spend hours agonizing over what you're going to say on each note. Just jot down your thoughts (be nice, now), thank the person for the gift, sign the card, and mail it.

- Wine and dine them. If you know a little something about wine — and none of your attendants has a drinking problem — invest in a good bottle of reserve wine for each of your attendants. Or buy them each a gift certificate to their favorite restaurant.

- A subscription to a favorite magazine. True, this would require personalization on your part (your maid of honor may not appreciate getting *Playboy* as much as your brother might), but magazine subscriptions are an easy—and affordable—gift.

- Fun yet practical gifts, such as kooky underwear or socks. Everyone wears them and on days when there's nothing in the house but dirty laundry (save for the brand-new panties and socks you gave them), your attendants will truly appreciate this gift.

- The purchase of the clothing the attendants will wear at your wedding. There's probably no better gift for your attendants than your footing their clothing bill.

Your Way or No Way

There's no way to avoid it. Weddings are big gift-giving affairs. Besides the gifts you get as husband and wife, you are expected to give gifts to the people who participate in your wedding. Parents are usually happy to have a corsage or a boutonniere, but you probably want to do a little something more when it comes to your attendants. Then there's the issue of writing thank-you notes. They are a must, so don't slack off. Here are the basics to keep in mind when it comes to gifts:

❧ Please register. It will make both your life and the lives of your guests easier. You will not be looked down upon for requesting certain wedding gifts. Registering has come to be an expected part of a wedding.

❧ You don't have to register at the same old store. Years ago, when brides were marrying boys from their hometowns, they registered at the china store in town and that was it. While many couples still go the traditional china-and-crystal route, your registry options are wide open now. Today, you can register for everything from a saw to a scuba-diving trip.

❧ When buying gifts for your attendants, make sure you choose something that is practical, useful, and even fun for your attendants. Keep their hobbies in mind when going gift shopping and don't be afraid to get a little creative.

❧ When receiving gifts, remember that you should write your thank-you note within six to eight weeks of receiving a gift. This is one task you do not want to put off, that is, unless you want to put off your family and friends. A great way to tackle the thank-you note writing marathon is to bring your notes with you on your honeymoon. Chances are you'll have a lot of downtime either in the airport or on the plane. Use this time to do your thank-you notes. You can write the notes, and your husband can address the envelopes. Or vice versa. Then, when you return from your trip, you can drop all of the notes in the mailbox. Even better, if you're honeymooning somewhere in the United States and you're sending notes to American guests, you can mail them directly from your honeymoon destination. The bottom line: don't forget to write your thank-you notes.

5

THE INSIDE SCOOP
ON INVITATIONS

The kind of invitations you choose to invite guests to your wedding says a lot about who you are as a couple and what kind of wedding you're going to have. Take my husband Bill and me. Because we were having a backyard brunch for our friends—and a casual one at that—we wanted our invitations to the reception to reflect the casual nature of the two of us and our party. So we chose a traditional-size card with a floral border, and printed our message in forest green. This was no ordinary ecru invitation with black engraved type oozing black-tie affair. No, our invitation screamed garden party, which was what we were having. To this day I talk about how thrilled I was when my guests started showing up at our party, all decked out for a garden party. Many of our female friends wore sundresses, sandals, and straw hats, and one enterprising male friend showed up in a linen blazer and navy blue walking shorts. Seeing our guests dress in the tenor of our party made us realize that the invitations we'd chosen had been perfect.

❧ Doing It Their Way ❧

"We designed our own invitation. Tom and I had been living together for five years when we decided to get married. We cut our mothers' smiling faces out of old snapshots and pasted them on the front of the invitation. Underneath their heads we wrote the following: 'Why are these women smiling?' When you opened the invitation, it said 'Because Tom and Sophie are finally getting married.' Then we gave all the details for the wedding. We had the type done at a typesetting shop and the invitations were printed at a print shop. It all looked kind of primitive, but since it was a kind of jokey invitation, we didn't mind."

—*Sophie and Tom, Dallas, Texas*

Brides and grooms today are having fun with their invitations, as I did, even if they're just personalizing the invitation in a small way. One of the reasons that you have so much freedom to do your invitations your way is "the guidelines for invitations aren't rigid for etiquette, form, and look" anymore, says Hannah Rodewald, owner of The Pleasure of Your Company, a stationer in Baltimore.

However, even without the former rigid standards for creating wedding invitations, Rodewald has seen definite trends in the kinds of invitations couples are choosing. Here is a rundown on some of the more modern touches and trends she's seeing in wedding invitations:

Larger invitations. Regular-size invitations, which most people think of when they think of wedding invitations, are called "embassy" or "clas-

sic." Larger invitations are called "royalty," probably because they were the
kind that royals used for their royal
weddings. Today, everyone but royals
are choosing the royalty invitations,
perhaps so that their parties will stand

out from other parties their guests are being invited to attend.

Inner envelopes. According to Rodewald, engaged couples originally
used inner envelopes for their wedding invitations during the pre–post
office days. "The invitations were hand-delivered, and the outer envelope
got very dirty during transit," says Rodewald. "People would discard the
soiled outer envelope but still have the clean inner envelope inside, with
the invited parties' names written on it. That tradition has been carried
down, and it's no longer totally relevant." However, just because these
envelopes are perhaps somewhat irrelevant doesn't mean you can't use
them—especially if you like the way they look.

Ribbons and bands. The couples who want to do something more
modern than the inner envelope are tending toward tying up the com-
ponents of their wedding invitation with ribbons that match the colors
of the wedding. Or, they may use a band of vellum paper that has the
guests' names written on the front, and it is secured in the back with a
sealing wax seal. Really, anything goes. For example, if you're having a
back-to-nature wedding, you could hold your wedding invitation together
with a piece of twine to create a real eye-opener for your guests.

Ecru-and-black invites are still on top. According to Rodewald, ecru
invitation paper with black lettering is still the most popular combina-

tion for weddings. Originally, that combination was reserved solely for very formal weddings, but like so much about wedding etiquette, the lines on that distinction have blurred. In fact, the lines of what is and isn't a formal wedding have become so fuzzy that brides planning a black-tie wedding often have to put "black-tie preferred" or "black-tie optional" to let guests know that most of the male guests at the wedding will be wearing black ties. However, if you're going to go for a seventies retro thing, you may want to put "blue tuxes preferred" on your invitation.

Actually, most etiquette mavens will tell you that it is in bad taste to tell your guests what to wear to your wedding. But why? You register for gifts, therefore telling your guests what to buy you for your wedding. So why can't you tell them what to wear, especially if you're having a theme wedding? For example, a couple having a Renaissance wedding will definitely want to tell their guests well in advance that certain costumes are preferred at the wedding. How much of an idiot would you feel if you showed up at a period wedding wearing a twentieth-century outfit?

Romantic is definitely in. "Romantic is soft colors, using periwinkle for ink instead of black, using real pressed flowers in the invitations, and having bows woven into the invitations," says Rodewald.

Motifs are big. Couples are choosing to put little decorative motifs on their wedding invitations as a way of giving it a personal touch. We're not talking wedding bells or doves here. Instead, the couple may have their monogram or a line drawing of their dog printed on the invitation. "We did the invitations for a wedding that was being held in the Maine woods, and we ended up putting a motif of a little green pine branch on the wedding invitation," Rodewald recalls. "We've used fleur-de-lis for Catholic weddings and four-leaf clovers for Irish weddings."

Metals are a must. Just as having a credit card in gold or platinum is a big thing now, so is having a hint of metal on your wedding invitation. The key, though, is *hint*. You do not want to overwhelm your guests with heavy metal. Instead, couples who want to accent their invitation with gold, silver, copper, bronze, or platinum may have the border of the card stock be in one of these metallic colors and that's it. Or they choose to have a motif on the invitation done in a metal hue.

Both parents get top billing. Traditionally, whoever is paying for the wedding gets top billing on an invitation. If it's the couple themselves, their names are displayed prominently. If it's the brides' parents, their names come first. With Jewish weddings, things are done a bit differently. Regardless of who is footing the bill, both sets of parents get mentioned on the invitation. "Because a Jewish wedding is seen as the union of two families, Jewish families include the groom's parents on the invitation," says Rodewald. Now, brides and grooms of varying religious backgrounds are realizing that they, too, want to mention all their par-

---

❧ Doing It Their Way ❧

"A professional printer did the formal invitations and a calligrapher addressed them. But we printed a weekend activity card and an RSVP postcard using our personal computer and inserted both with our invitations. The activity cards gave guests a heads up on what was planned for our weekend wedding, and the postcards allowed guests to check the activities they wanted to attend." —*Kelli and Scott, Houston, Texas*

ents' names on the invitations, and they are. Of course, this can make for some serious crowding on a small invitation (which may be why more brides and grooms are choosing the royalty invitation), so Rodewald suggests using your instinct and retaining good taste when writing an invitation that includes all the parents' names. If you find that you need two cards to include everyone, maybe it's better to include only the names of the couple getting married.

Rsvp cards have changed.   It used to be that when you were invited to a wedding, the RSVP card included a line on which you could write your name and check off whether you would attend or not. How boring. "A lot of today's brides feel that the fill-in-the-blank card is insulting, and they want the fun of reading something on the card instead of just looking at check marks," says Rodewald, who makes many of the RSVP cards blank so that the guest can write whatever he or she pleases in response to the invitation. Of course, some guest may not be comfortable with this newfangled approach or understand how it works, so you may want to include a printed line or two on the RSVP card suggesting that the guest write his or her name in and a personal note, if he or she pleases. That way people won't misunderstand the concept of the blank RSVP card and send it back to you blank. Now what good would that do you?

Computer calligraphy.   While Rodewald says calligraphers are alive and well all over the United States, more and more tech-savvy brides and grooms are investing in font programs for their computers and generating their own calligraphy for their envelopes or, if they're doing their invitations themselves, for the entire package.

Save the Date cards are a must.   With brides and grooms hailing from different places these days (as opposed to the old-fashioned notion of the

---

~≪ *Doing It Her Way* ≫~

"Because our wedding was a weekend away, I did a Save the Date card. With our wedding being held at a winery, I wanted to find stationery for the Save the Date card that would fit with our theme. I ended up printing the Save the Date card myself on my computer after I found this great vellum paper with a gold border of grapes on it."

—*Marisa, New York City*

---

hometown boy marrying the hometown girl), suddenly they find themselves with guest lists featuring lots of out-of-town friends and relatives. "Many times they have to get regrets in before they can invite other people," says Rodewald. While the Save the Date card doesn't ask for a response per se, "it opens up the topic for discussion," she says. Plus, since you're going to send your wedding invitations out only six to eight weeks before your wedding, you may want a prior estimate of how many people will or will not attend your wedding, before the final invitations go out.

Rodewald suggests that if you can swing it, try to send your Save the Date card a few weeks before most people mail their holiday cards. "That way as you get holiday greetings from these various people, you'll probably get a written note back in response to your Save the Date card that will let you know whether or not so-and-so will be able to attend your upcoming wedding," she says.

Save the Date cards are also very practical when travel arrangements or hotel reservations are involved in the wedding plans. "We did a Save the Date card for a Nantucket wedding the next summer, and when you do a wedding in Nantucket, you have to make ferry arrangements in January," says Rodewald. Because of the time sensitivity of the guests' travel plans, this couple mailed their Save the Date cards before Christmas so guests who would be coming to their Nantucket wedding would have enough time to reserve a spot on the ferry.

❧ Doing It Their Way ❧

"Instead of sending out formal invitations, we sent out four-page flyers with valuable information relevant to our wedding in Lake Tahoe. We included hotel prices at a variety of levels (luxury, moderate, or economy rates), ski prices, movie theater schedules, and directions to outlet stores. We also included a schedule of events for the entire weekend."

—*Susan and Jim, Silverthorne, Colorado*

Your Way or No Way

The sky is the limit when it comes to your wedding invitations. You can go the traditional route if you're a traditional person, or you can print your wedding invitations on funky paper that fits the theme of your wedding. Just make sure you keep the basics in mind. Tell your guests who is getting married, where, and when. The invitation isn't the place to recount your life story together. Save that for the wedding program. Also keep in mind that if you're planning a wedding far in advance, you'll want to send a Save the Date card. Not only will this card (and the responses you get from it) help you plan and budget your guest list, but it will also help your guests make affordable travel arrangements for your wedding.

~ 6 ~

CREATIVE CEREMONIES

Some of the most memorable wedding ceremonies I've ever attended were those that truly reflected the people who were becoming husband and wife that day. Making your ceremony personal takes just a small effort on your behalf. For example, one friend, a devout Anglophile who probably wishes she had lived during the Elizabethan age (instead of in modern times), sprinkled passages from Shakespeare's quintessential love story *Romeo and Juliet* throughout the wedding ceremony. If you were to know this woman, you'd know that reciting lines from the play's balcony scene to her soon-to-be husband was the most personal way for her to express her love—and very touching for those in the audience.

At another wedding ceremony I attended, the bride and groom asked the guests to recite vows to them. In these vows, they asked us to help them pursue their marriage and to be part of their support system. It was

⭒ *Doing It Their Way* ⭒

"My husband and I met at an audition for a comedy improvisational group. If you've ever seen the television show *Whose Line Is It Anyway?* you'll know the kind of improv we do. Kip proposed to me at the end of one of our shows (obviously we both got hired) by using the rest of the cast to perform different skits involving marriage proposals. In order to keep the theme going, we decided to have an entertainment-themed wedding ceremony.

"We named our wedding 'Two Flew Over the Cuckoo's Nest,' which was the heading of our invitation. It looked more like a movie poster than an invitation. Our wedding program resembled a movie script, including a list of cast members (i.e., the bridal party and guests).

"When guests arrived at the ceremony, we had paparazzi (really Kip's brothers and sisters) greet them with Polaroid cameras. After their pictures were taken, we had the guests autograph them. These signed pictures comprise our guest book. After the guests were seated and just before the ceremony began, we had the MGM movie theme play—it's a trumpet fanfare.

"Our actual ceremony utilized an improv game called 'Pick a Line.' This involves the audience writing a line of dialogue on a piece of paper, and then the actors read the lines randomly as part of a scene. In our case, our wedding guests wrote what they felt would be appropriate vows for us to say. We chose five of the lines as part of our vows. It was a really fun way to get married." —*Debra and Kip, Marina del Ray, California*

a special moment for me when the guests responded "We will" to the various questions the couple posed; I couldn't help but feel truly part of the marriage of these two people.

Still another personal moment occurred at a wedding I attended with my husband Bill. I'd never actually met the bride, Jenny, but she was one of Bill's best friends during college. As she walked down the aisle on her father's arm, she stopped to greet almost every person whom she passed. She was so committed to her desire to welcoming everyone to her wedding that she'd even taken the trouble to learn my name. I practically fell off my pew when she stopped, said "Hello" to Bill, and then said, "It's nice to finally meet you, Leah."

⤙ Doing It Their Way ⤚

"We had the entire congregation hold hands during the prayer where the congregation pledges to support the couple, and we took communion. The minister had cut the bread into a heart shape and held it up for everyone to see." —*Tina and Richard, Long Beach, California*

"After the ceremony during the recessional, I knew everyone would be crying and very emotional. To break up the tension, I had our musician segue from the traditional wedding music to the theme from *Mission: Impossible*. Everyone laughed and relaxed and joined in the celebratory mood."

—*Julia, Bristol, Pennsylvania*

Using Your Program Wisely

I'm not saying that you need to commit to memory the names of all your guests and greet each one as Jenny did, but it would be nice if you could do a little something to make your guests feel more a part of the ceremony they're witnessing. A great way to give your guests the inside scoop on your courtship is to write a brief history of your relationship and print it in the program. That way as your guests are arriving, being seated, and waiting for the ceremony to begin, they can get up-to-date on exactly who you both are (if they don't already know), how you met, and how you came to be married this particular day. Remember: not everyone who attends your wedding will know you as well as, say, your best friend or your mother. So it isn't unreasonable to offer them some additional information about yourselves. And since there will probably be some members of the audience who already know all your deep dark secrets, make sure you write your program in an entertaining style. That way, even if they're reading stuff that's familiar to them, at least they'll enjoy reading it.

The program can serve another use: to explain all the parts of the ceremony that might have a special meaning for you, but whose significance might otherwise be lost on your guests. For example, if I had to plan my wedding ceremony all over again, I most definitely would have included the song "It Had to Be You" by Harry Connick, Jr., which appears on the soundtrack to *When Harry Met Sally*. That movie has a multitude of meanings in Bill's and my relationship. First, it was one of the first movies we saw together when we were dating. Second, the extended friendship between Meg Ryan and Billy Crystal (who play

Sally and Harry, respectively) that gradually grew into love is quite parallel to what happened with Bill and me. And, third, the movie's soundtrack is one of our favorites and in a sense became the soundtrack of our lives while we were dating. For instance, the instrumental version of "Winter Wonderland" graced our outgoing answering machine message during our first holiday together. If we'd included any of the movie's songs in our ceremony, we would have used the program as the vehicle for explaining the music's significance to us as a couple.

❧ Doing It Her Way ❧

"My grandmother is an amazing and award-winning quilter, so I'd always imagined that she would make my *huppah* when I got married. As soon as I got engaged, I asked her if she would quilt a *huppah* for me, and she agreed! I left the design up to her, but told her what colors we'd be using in the wedding. She designed a gorgeous appliquéd *huppah* that has a wreath of roses, in different colors of pink. She even took scraps of fabric from the bridesmaids' dresses, and used that fabric in the *huppah*. It's beautiful, and I'll be so proud to have it as part of our wedding. After the ceremony, we'll display the *huppah* so that our guests can see it close-up."

—*Callie, Hoboken, New Jersey*

Another great use for the program is to help guests understand the religious significance of something in the ceremony, especially if they are not of the same religion as the bride and groom. In Jewish ceremonies, for example, the bride and groom are married underneath a *huppah*, or a bridal canopy, which is a piece of cloth held aloft by four poles. The *huppah* symbolizes the home the bride and groom will make together after they are married. Supposedly, the *huppah* is not a sturdy contraption—it could collapse at any time—in order to show how fragile a marriage between two people can be if they are not careful. The symbolism here is wonderful, and I wouldn't be surprised if non-Jewish couples chose to use it in their ceremonies. But the *huppah*'s significance isn't entirely obvious. I was raised Jewish, and I didn't even know what the *huppah* was supposed to stand for until I started researching this book! So if you're going to have one at your ceremony, explain its significance to your guests by writing a little something in your program about it.

❧ *Doing It Her Way* ❧

"My father died a few years before I got married, and I knew I wanted to incorporate something about him into the ceremony. My father had a wonderful *tallis* (prayer shawl) that was made in Israel. The rabbi who was officiating at our ceremony suggested that my future father-in-law wear it during the ceremony, which he did. At one point, the rabbi took the *tallis* off my father-in-law and wrapped it around my husband and me as a way of bringing both of our fathers together with us. It was a lovely gesture."

—*Marisa, New York City*

Another religious symbol that many people may not understand that often shows up at weddings, is the unity candle. A standard at Christian and Catholic weddings, its use is slowly creeping across religious lines. Why does a couple choose to light a unity candle at their wedding? Sure, everyone looks good in soft candlelight and it adds a romantic and mysterious mood to the ceremony, but there's more to the candle than that. Unity candles generally symbolize the individual flames of the bride and groom joining to become one flame. A nice touch to add is having a parent literally pass the torch or flame of life from himself or herself to the child getting married and then have the children light their own candle using the flames from both their families. If you'll be doing something special with the unity candle, explain your choices in your program for your guests' benefit.

Writing Your Own Vows

One of the most common ways that people personalize their wedding ceremony is by writing their own vows. While it's a noble undertaking to script the vows you will say when you become husband and wife, you should keep a number of guidelines in mind as you put your pen to paper (or fingers to the computer keyboard, as the case may be).

• Remember your audience. "In writing wedding vows, you have to keep in mind that you're addressing more than just your partner. You're also addressing the people attending the wedding, and that may entail friends, family, work colleagues, and even strangers," says Peter Marston, Ph.D., a professor of communications studies at California State University at Northridge and an expert in the communication of romantic love. "You

Marriage Memoirs

And you thought *you* were a modern woman. According to Susan J. Gordon's book *Wedding Days* (William Morrow and Co., 1998), *Little House on the Prairie* author Laura Ingalls was proposed to in 1885 when she was 17. The man who wanted to marry her was Almanzo Wilder. When Almanzo proposed marriage, Laura agreed, but with the following contingency, says Gordon: "As long as the word *obey* was omitted from her vows, because she didn't think she should obey anyone 'against [her] better judgment.'"

have to find a balance to what is appropriate to say in a wedding ceremony and what is useful for the audience to hear." Using a romantic passage from a well-known work of literature, such as *Romeo and Juliet,* is most appropriate for a wedding and something most of your guests will appreciate. Writing your own vows and using bizarre metaphors to describe your love for one another probably isn't appropriate.

• Examine your reasons for wanting to write your own wedding vows. Are you a complete control freak and must choreograph every moment of your wedding, down to the actual words you will say during the ceremony? Or are there sentimental reasons for wanting to script your vows? Just remember that writing your own vows has to be a decision that both of you make, not only one of you.

• Dr. Marston, who researches how couples communicate love, says that how one person expresses love—and wants love expressed back—may not be the same as how the other person in the relationship expresses and receives love. For example, a man who wants to hear "I love you" over and over again may decide that self-written wedding vows with multiple expressions of these three little words is the best way for him to show his soon-to-be wife how much he loves her. But if public displays of affection make her uncomfortable, vows where "I love you" is almost chanted may make her want to run screaming from the ceremony. "You have to learn and negotiate ways of expressing your love to the other person," he says. "You could increase the value of sentiment of your wedding vows by paying attention to how your partner receives love." So if your partner is shy and would feel uncomfortable with elaborately written expressions of love in your vows, why not offer one or two self-composed sentences instead and then leave the rest of the vows up to the officiant?

I Do Data

A 1999 Wedding Trends Survey from *Bridal Guide* magazine reveals that:

- 65 percent of couples write their own vows.
- 72 percent light a unity candle.
- 59 percent have a relative or friend perform at the wedding.
- 44 percent design their own wedding program.

• Keep the tenor of your wedding ceremony in mind when writing vows. What this means is if you're having a fairly traditional Roman Catholic ceremony, for example, inserting a reading from an Aerosmith song, no matter how touching it is to you, would seem completely out of place. I'm not exaggerating here. Sometimes a bride and groom lose their collective head and don't stop and really think about what they're composing for their vows. "I once attended a traditional Jewish wedding, where the bride and groom wrote their own vows. At one point the bride said to the groom, 'You're the chocolate on my ice cream sundae,'" recalls

Sandra E. Lamb, author of *How to Write It: A Complete Guide to Everything You'll Ever Write* (Ten Speed Press, 1999). "Everything else about the ceremony was very traditional, but these vows just stood out like, 'What were they thinking?'" Do you want to look back at your wedding video, watch the part of the tape with your ceremony on it, and cringe each time your self-composed vows tumble out of your mouth? Keep this in mind as you summon your vow-writing muse.

• Shorter is better. "I always say that people don't know how to edit," says Lamb. It's better to make your vows be two or three minutes of emotionally charged, sentimental prose rather than twenty minutes of utter drivel and rambling. Before you finalize your vows, have someone else read them—your bridesmaids, a close friend—who will give you an unbiased and honest opinion about what you've written.

In addition, make sure you read your vows out loud before finalizing them. Not only will this give you the chance to see how long you'll actually be speaking your vows (in case you want to cut the time down), but "speaking out loud can turn things up that sound silly," suggests Lamb. "You may have repeated a word where all of a sudden it stands out and sounds funny, or maybe you sound too formal or informal."

Also, before you commit your vows to memory, make sure you run them by the pastor, priest, or rabbi who will be marrying you. Doing so is an act of common courtesy since you'll be saying these vows during what is, in essence, his or her ceremony. Plus, it will give the officiant the chance to nix anything that is inappropriate. "He may tell you that something you want to say is not in keeping with church doctrine or whatever," explains Lamb.

- Practice, practice, practice. Make sure you and your partner practice your vows long before your wedding rehearsal, "because by then it's too far into the game to make changes," advises Lamb. Whether or not you memorize your vows is entirely up to you. Personally, I wouldn't want the added pressure, but people like Lamb believe that working toward memorization gives you "a chance to really think about what you're saying." If you do decide to go the memorization route, make sure someone (the officiant? your maid of honor?) has your script on hand in case you get stage fright or a mental block and need to be prompted as to what to say. If you don't have a script on hand "and you stumble or miss a passage, you're going to have to ad lib," says Lamb. "But if you get stuck for a word and your script is nearby, someone can give you a prompt." Lamb suggests typing your script, using double line spaces and large margins so it's easy to follow along.

While writing your own vows is a noble undertaking, you don't have to do it if you don't want to. Being responsible for what everyone in the wedding is going to say is a huge responsibility, and it will add more pressure to you during an already stressful time. Choosing readings for others to do makes a lot of sense, but if you're uncomfortable being a wordsmith, then leave the vows up to the person who will be officiating at the ceremony.

Creating an Interfaith Ceremony

One of the challenges that faced Bill and me when we were planning our wedding was the fact that he was raised Catholic and I was raised Jew-

---

~≪ NEWS YOU CAN USE: INTERFAITH WEDDINGS ≫~

Finding a priest or pastor to officiate at an interfaith wedding ceremony is usually easier than finding a rabbi to do the same. The Dovetail Institute for Interfaith Family Resources, a nonprofit organization that helps Jewish and Christian partners explore an interfaith household, can help. They have contacts at houses of worship around the country with officiants willing to preside over an interfaith wedding. For more information, call 800-530-1596 or E-mail Dovetail at DI-IFR@bardstown.com.

---

ish. Because of our differing religions, we couldn't be married in either house of worship—his because I couldn't take communion during mass and mine because most rabbis won't marry a couple when the Jewish member of that couple is marrying outside the faith. To find a religious officiant to perform our wedding meant having to go outside of both religions, and we ended up with a civil ceremony.

"One of the first hurdles you'll face as an interfaith couple planning a wedding—and potentially one of the hardest to surmount—is the choice of an officiant for your wedding ceremony," says Joan Hawxhurst, author of *Interfaith Wedding Ceremonies: Samples and Sources* (Dovetail Publishing, 1996) and editor of "Dovetail," a newsletter by and for Jewish and Christian families. Both publications come from Dovetail Institute, a nonprofit organization that helps Jewish and Christian partners explore the spiritual and religious dimensions of an interfaith household.

With more and more couples today marrying someone of a different religion—a recent National Jewish Population Study found that nearly half of all Jewish people were marrying someone of another religion—the issue of planning an interfaith wedding is becoming top-of-mind for a number of engaged couples these days. With that in mind, Hawxhurst offers the following advice so you won't lose your mind as you plan an interfaith wedding ceremony:

• Choose one religion to represent at your ceremony. If I could have found a rabbi to marry us, Bill would have agreed in a second to have a Jewish wedding. One of the reasons that I married Bill is he doesn't see his religion as being "better" than mine or vice versa—meaning that one would rule out over the other for all our life decisions, including how we would be married.

Sometimes choosing whose religion you'll use at the ceremony can dig up a whole host of unresolved issues you may both have about your respective religious backgrounds and how you're going to recognize each in your marriage, let alone your wedding. In my opinion, if the person you're marrying has preconceived notions of his or her religion winning out over yours—and therefore insists that it is his or her religion that must be used at the wedding and forever after—then your issue isn't finding a religion to be married in but rather that you need to work out some serious stuff with this person before you tie the knot. "Successful interfaith couples have one thing in common," Hawxhurst reports. "They have open-minded, respectful dialogue about the issues they face when it comes to religion."

• Blend both religions into your wedding ceremony. It is very common these days to attend a wedding during which the couple is married under

❧ *Doing It Their Way* ❧

"Because my husband Martin's background is Quaker, we wanted a very simple wedding. Therefore, we decided to get married in our backyard. Although we didn't have a Quaker wedding per se, we put together our own ceremony that included readings (mostly from non-religious literature) and other touches that reflected Martin's heritage. But first, to understand our choices of music and readings, you need to know a bit about who we are.

"At the time we got married, we had moved from New York City to a small farm in northeastern Pennsylvania. For Martin, who grew up on a farm in Ohio, it was a little like coming home. He finally was able to garden again—he grew all of the vegetables for the wedding dinner. For me, a life-long New Yorker, it was my own attempt at Thoreau's Walden Pond.

"In fact, one of the readings we chose for our ceremony included a passage from *Walden*, which talked about the path we had taken together that had brought us to where we are now. We also had a friend sing 'Simple Gifts,' a traditional Quaker hymn, and, in keeping with my New York heritage, he also sang 'One Hand, One Heart' from *West Side Story*.

"Another special touch was we had a Quaker wedding certificate, which was signed by all of our one hundred or so guests, including the children. We now have that certificate framed and hanging on our bedroom wall. It's a wonderful reminder of that wonderful day."

—*Emily and Martin, Milansville, Pennsylvania*

a *huppah* (a Jewish tradition) and then lights a unity candle together (a Christian tradition). Another way to have both religions represented in a Jewish-Christian wedding is to have the ceremony be Christian in most respects, but have the groom break a glass at the end of the ceremony like people do at a Jewish wedding.

• Have two ceremonies. If you choose to be married in a church and then again in a synagogue, understand that only the first ceremony you participate in will be legal, says Hawxhurst. "The second ceremony is technically a 'blessing' of the marriage," she says.

• Find a neutral religion for your ceremony. One of the options Bill and I considered was being married by an Episcopal priest in an Episcopal church. This way our ceremony would have many of the Christian traditions Bill knew and loved without any of the strict doctrines of a Roman Catholic ceremony. Likewise, the Episcopal priest we met was willing to meld some Jewish traditions into the ceremony to represent my faith. "Some interfaith couples choose to be married in the Unitarian Universalist Church or the Ethical Cultural Society, because these traditions are inclusive and embracing of both Jewish and Christian beliefs," says Hawxhurst.

• Have a civil ceremony. If you've attempted to exercise all your religious options—and all the obstacles you've faced have made you both consider becoming atheist—then having a civil ceremony is probably best.

1 Do Data

Eighty-seven percent of wedding ceremonies take place in a church, chapel, or synagogue, according to the Association of Bridal Consultants. The average cost for the clergy, rabbi, church, chapel, or synagogue is about $140.

Traditions with a Twist: Attendants with a Pedigree

If it weren't for her dog, Maria never would have met her husband. "I'd written a book on great places to take your dog in the San Francisco Bay area, and Craig was going to interview me for a television program," Maria recalls. Because it seemed appropriate, Craig brought his springer spaniel Nisha along to the interview. Nisha was immediately smitten with Maria's dog Joe, an Airedale terrier, and soon so was Maria with Craig.

"The dogs were a vital part of our lives, so how could we leave them at home when we said our vows?" Maria asks. The answer? They couldn't. Nisha was the flower girl, with a ring of purple flowers around her collar, and Joe was the ring bearer. "I made a purple velvet pouch for the ring and attached it to his collar," she says. Because it proved challenging to find a location that would allow the canine attendants, Maria and Craig ended up getting married on a fishing boat as it sailed underneath the Golden Gate Bridge. Unfortunately, Joe had yet to develop his sea legs and felt sick for most of the ceremony. "He hid his head under my dress, so all of our pictures have Joe with his head between my knees," jokes Maria.

All joking aside, having your dog participate in your wedding can be serious business if you're a dog lover. Wendy Ballard, publisher of "DogGone," the newsletter about fun places to go and cool stuff to do with your dog, offers the following tips for including your dog in your wedding:

- Consider an outdoor ceremony, since most churches or synagogues won't allow a dog inside. A wedding at home is best, but if you decide to have your ceremony at a public park, understand you may need to apply for a special permit for the dog.

- Have your dog attend obedience classes well in advance of your wedding so he or she will be behaved on the big day. You wouldn't want your dog jumping up and leaving muddy paw prints on your wedding dress!

- Dogs may not like the music you play at your wedding, and having your dog run howling from the sound of the harp playing during your ceremony is not a good thing. "Expose your dog to the sound in advance," advises Ballard.
- Train your dog to act as a ring bearer, as Maria did with Joe, or the flower girl, if you choose. If you do decide to have the dog carry the rings, however "make sure your dog is securely leashed at all times so as not to bolt with the precious bands," Ballard warns.
- Designate one person to be the dog watcher during the wedding so you don't have to worry. In addition, make sure the dog is walked before the ceremony begins. Says Ballard, "There is more than one incident on record of a dog answering nature's call mid-ceremony!"

No matter who you choose to officiate at your ceremony or what level of religious symbolism you decide to incorporate, remember these wise words from Hawxhurst: "Intermarried couples who spend time and energy to create a ceremony that incorporates what is important to each partner from their respective religious traditions usually feel that their wedding day has formed a firm base on which to build a life together."

Neat Places to Tie the Knot

While houses of worship continue to be the most popular places for couples to get married, your options are virtually unlimited when it comes to choosing your ceremony locale. To save time and money, choose a place where you can have your ceremony and your reception. That way you won't have to pay two rental fees and your guests won't have to travel from one location to the next. If this idea appeals to you, check out hotels, country clubs, and traditional reception halls. All usually have space to accommodate ceremonies and receptions.

If you're willing to make a little effort to keep your wedding under one roof, consider having your wedding at home. That's what Emily and Martin of Milansville, Pennsylvania, did. They got married and celebrated their union in their backyard. But make sure that you follow the old Boy Scout motto and be prepared. "Or course all the money in the world couldn't have prevented the downpour that occurred right as I was walking down the aisle," recalls Emily. Luckily the couple had invested in a tent.

If you're looking for a really creative place to hold your ceremony (and possibly your reception as well), consider the following:

• On a boat. There are a number of yacht companies that charter their boats especially for weddings. Many of them are winterized so that even if you get married, let's say, in Boston in the dead of winter, you'll still be able to enjoy your wedding without freezing.

• At a firehouse. A number of fire stations have refurbished their buildings and transformed open spaces into event spaces. These spaces usually rent for very little money, and they definitely offer a unique venue for getting married.

• In a public park. When David and Julie of Bristol, Pennsylvania, got engaged, they agreed that there was one place in their hometown (they grew up in Bristol) where they'd like to become husband and wife: the public park along the Delaware River. There they'd had their first date, shared their first kiss, and visited on the night they got engaged. Not only

‿❧ *Doing It Their Way* ❧‿

"When you're planning a civil wedding ceremony in March in Minnesota, you don't have many options. So we got married at The Chapel of Love, the only wedding chapel in an enclosed shopping mall. It's in the Mall of America in Bloomington, Minnesota. We had about sixty guests who all dressed formally, and we were married by a minister.

"Bored with the hum-drum unity candle ceremony, Alec and I decided to do something different. We made our first dance part of our wedding ceremony. We danced to 'Have You Ever Really Loved a Woman' by Bryan Adams from the *Don Juan DeMarco* soundtrack. We danced a rumba, and we talked the whole time. Everyone asked us what we talked about, and I have no idea. It was just so beautiful to be together. The guests all commented that they were very touched that we added this special dance to our ceremony. Doing something unique like that made the day even more special."

—*Erin and Alec, St. Paul, Minnesota*

was the park available for rent for weddings, but because it was maintained by a civic organization, in this case the Lions Club, the only fee they had to pay was an optional donation to the organization (they sent $100). I've heard of other couples getting married in public parks where the fee was extremely reasonable or nonexistent.

• At a historic home. When Bill and I were searching for a place to hold our wedding, we checked out a historic home in the town where we grew up. It offered soaring ceilings and gorgeous hardwood floors, and it would have cost about $500 to rent. Two problems: it didn't have sufficient electrical outlets (the wiring was old and outdated, our caterer told us), and there was no air-conditioning. Considering we were planning a late June wedding in New York, the latter was a must. Even though the historic home we looked at didn't work out for us, in general they are great locations for weddings.

When Therese and Michael of San Jose, California, tied the knot, they chose a historic home as the setting for their ceremony. "We got married in the small garden of a restored Victorian home in a park on the San Francisco Bay," Therese recalls. "Since we're outdoorsy people, the garden seemed appropriate. Plus, if it had rained, we could have moved the wedding inside. Knowing that gave me peace of mind."

• At a museum or zoo. Believe it or not, many of this country's best-known museums and zoos are available for private affairs. For example, if you wanted to, you could rent The New York Aquarium in Coney Island, Brooklyn, for your wedding ceremony and reception. The Aquarium has space that can accommodate parties of up to five hundred people. Think about it: you could exchange vows in front of dolphins and penguins, as well as your guests. Now that would make for an affair to remember!

• At a winery. While there has been some recent controversy in California's Napa and Sonoma Valleys about private events at wineries, in many other places around the country where wine is made (Virginia, upstate New York, Long Island, for example), wineries welcome couples who wish to be married and celebrate on their grounds.

Flower Power

Thanks to the influence of Martha Stewart, brides are even more into flowers at their wedding ceremonies than they have been in days gone by, says Nathaniel Shell, owner of Nathaniel's Flowers Etc., in Dallas. What Stewart has been pushing lately—and what brides are picking up on—are hand-tied bouquets filled with wildflowers. "You just don't see exotic flowers anymore," says Shell. Good-bye orchids, hello daisies. "Hand-tied bouquets are the most cost-effective," says Shell, "because

---

⤜ NEWS YOU CAN USE: THE MEANING OF FLOWERS ⤏

A great way to add a personal touch to the bouquets in your wedding is to consider what different flowers mean. According to Shell, here are some flowers and what they symbolize:

Carnation—lasting fidelity and
 deep love
Daisy—faith and cheer
Forget-me-not—true love
Gardenia—joy
Holly—foresight
Iris—faith and wisdom
Jonquil—affection returned

Lily of the valley—happiness
Orange blossoms—fertility and
 marriage
Purple lilac—first love
Red and white roses
 (together)—unity
Tulip—perfect lover
Violet—faithfulness

they're not labor-intensive for me." Plus, they look great at both formal and informal weddings.

Bouquets are so popular that they're replacing corsages and baskets of flowers that mothers, grandmothers, and flower girls traditionally received at weddings. "Instead of a basket of petals, flower girls are carrying miniature versions of the bride's bouquet," says Shell. "The same goes for mothers and grandmothers." Shell also uses lots of flowers with bold colors, such as bright yellow sunflowers.

What makes a florist like Shell versatile and creative is the fact that he hand-picks all the flowers in his store by visiting the local wholesale flower market on a regular basis. "A lot of florists, generally speaking, pre-order everything they use," says Shell. While this may be great if you've got your heart set on red tulips (even if they're not in season), it also means that your floral bill can get out of hand. By using a florist who chooses the freshest blooms available, you're assured that you're working with someone who truly understands how to work with flowers—and work with any bride's budget.

A budget-conscious and sensitive florist will understand when you say "I have a $500 floral budget." He or she will find you everything you need for your ceremony and make sure the bill comes in under $500. A sensitive florist will also offer you ways to stretch your flower dollar, such as finding floral arrangements that can do double duty. That is, first you use them at the ceremony for decoration, and then you bring them to the reception as centerpieces. At one wedding Shell did, the bride chose to decorate the pews in the church with dried-flower wreaths. Those same wreaths showed up later at the reception as table decorations.

As with any vendor you hire for your wedding, make sure you like your florist. (Why give a jerk work? He or she will just make your life miserable.) Also, make sure the florist respects your budget and can show you pictures of flowers he or she had done for previous weddings. Finally, make sure the florist comes highly recommended, either from people you know or from previous wedding customers.

With This Ring

The one part of your wedding ceremony that you'll carry with you for the rest of your life, but you'll probably plan for the least, is your wedding rings. I know this lack of planning was true for me.

When Bill proposed to me, he offered an emerald-cut diamond, offset with two baguettes, all of which were set in platinum. It was the ring his mother had worn when she was married, and her mother before her. This was more than an engagement ring; it was a family heirloom and a gorgeous piece of jewelry to boot. During my entire engagement period, I wore the ring with perfectly manicured nails, and I cleaned it regularly so the stone sparkled in the light. As Bill and I began to plan our wedding, we kept putting off the task of buying our rings. Everything else seemed so daunting that figuring out which wedding bands we would wear for the rest of our lives paled by comparison. When it finally came time to buy the rings—our ceremony was just a few days away—we were so emotionally and financially spent that we bought the cheapest ring for me that we could find. It was a plain white-gold band, and it looked perfectly nice next to my platinum engagement ring. And the price was right—about $100.

I Do Data

The average length of an engagement is thirteen and a half months, so says the Association of Bridal Consultants.

While the white gold and platinum worked well together for the first few years of our marriage, a funny thing happened on the way to our five-year anniversary: the white gold started to look more gold than white. According to jewelry experts, this color change is completely normal, especially when compared with a platinum engagement ring. Platinum is one of the hardest and most true metals. It won't bend, nick, or change color over time. Gold, on the other hand, is more malleable. It gets scratched and it changes color, especially white gold.

That said, when you buy your wedding bands, make sure you buy something that works well with your engagement ring—especially if you'll be wearing the two rings together on the same finger. If you have a platinum engagement ring like I do, get a platinum wedding band. Likewise, if your engagement ring is set in gold, it would be best if your wedding band was, too. In addition, don't put off buying your rings to the last minute. Many jewelers do not sell rings off the rack, so to speak, or out of the display case. When you order a ring, you're getting a custom-made design, and custom-made anything takes time. Therefore, it's not unreasonable for you to start shopping for your wedding band as soon as you set a date. Remember: you'll be wearing this ring for years to come. Buy wisely.

Rehearsal Dinner

Most brides and grooms have a run-through of their ceremony the night before their actual wedding, and then follow the practice session with a rehearsal dinner. This dinner is traditionally the first time the bridal party gets together to meet, eat, and gossip, and if the bride and groom have any gifts to give out to their attendants, they do it at the dinner. But, between you and me, this all sounds very ho-hum and boring. Thankfully, nowadays it's okay to use a lot of creativity, and brides I know are finding fun things their bridal party can do together in lieu of the same old rehearsal dinner.

Take Kelli and Scott who are tying the knot in Louisville, Kentucky, (see their anecdote in Chapter 9, "Weddings Away"). Because they have so many friends and family coming into town for their wedding, they have expanded their rehearsal dinner to a bona fide event to which all their guests are invited. They are taking everyone to the Louisville Slugger museum for a dinner hosted by Scott's parents. Then, because they rented the entire place for the evening, all the guests can enjoy the museum's hands-on exhibits in addition to the dinner.

If you'll be having a lot of guests in town—or even if it's just going to be your bridal party—why not do something fun for your rehearsal dinner? Is your favorite baseball team in town? Get tickets for everyone so you can take them out to the ball game. Not only will you have fun and do something different, but you won't have to worry about spending tons of money on catering another event (although you should probably pick up the tab for hot dogs and beer). Are you getting married in winter? Why not take everyone ice-skating or for a sleigh ride?

What about doing something very touristy for your guests who may never have been to your city before? If you're getting married in New York, why not take everyone to the top of the Empire State Building or take a ride on the Staten Island ferry. In Chicago, spend the night before your wedding at Navy Pier where, during warm weather months, there's an amusement park and free live music. Tying the knot in Cleveland? See if the Rock and Roll Museum and Hall of Fame will stay open late so you can all take a trip down musical memory lane.

Once you put your mind to coming up with new and nifty things to do instead of a normal rehearsal dinner, you'll be surprised with the ideas you come up with.

Traditions with a Twist: The Modern Guest Book

Everyone thinks they have to have a guest book at their wedding. It seems like the perfect way to record everyone who attended your ceremony, and the perfect place for people to record their good wishes for you. But as one who has manned a guest book at a wedding, I can tell you that wedding guests, by and large, are not the most creative folk, and without any prompting, they'll simply sign their name in your guest book and be on their way. How boring.

Why not jazz up your guest book potential by doing something that isn't quite a guest book but allows you to record who came to your wedding and their wishes for you? Two brides I know did similar yet different things with their guest books. Instead of having a book for guests to sign, they sent with each invitation a square of cloth on which the invited guest could write his or her name and, if inspired, any good wishes for the couple. Those squares were then sent back with the RSVP card and sewn together to make, in one instance, a quilt for the couple's bed, and, in another instance, a *huppah* that the couple used at their wedding. What was great about having the cloth squares sent to guests in the invitations was that even the people who couldn't attend the wedding were able to contribute to the project.

Another couple took their engagement photo, blew it up to become a large-size photograph, and mounted it on a mat board. At the wedding, they asked guests to sign their names and write anything their hearts desired on the mat board. After the wedding was over, the couple framed the photograph and hung it in their living room as a constant reminder of their wedding day.

The possibilities are endless for how you can capture your guests' good wishes without using a traditional guest book. How about investing in an instant camera, asking a friend with a steady hand and some knowledge of how to work a camera to photograph each person as he or she enters the ceremony? Then, hand each guest his or her picture and ask the guest to write a little something on it. Once the messages are written, have all the guests place their photographs in a designated basket or envelope. By the end of the ceremony, you will have collected a photographic memento of each guest along with his or her good wishes for you. You can put all of these photos in a special wedding scrapbook.

Why not have fun with how you record your guests at your wedding? If you really want to have the traditional guest book, then do it. There's nothing wrong with it. But if you're looking to do something a little creative, let your imagination be your guide as you figure out exactly how you want to do your guest book your way.

❧ *Doing It Her Way* ❧

"Following the receiving line, our guests will gather outside where ushers will distribute loose birdseed from galvanized steel buckets, which we purchased inexpensively at Restoration Hardware. I like the idea of the loose birdseed rather than the tied bundles of rice."

—*Kelli, Houston, Texas*

❧ NEWS YOU CAN USE: TOSS OUT THE RICE ❧

For centuries, wedding guests have tossed rice at the exiting bride and groom—that is, in the North, the tossing is done as they leave their ceremony, and in the South, rice is tossed as the happy couple leaves the reception. However, many sites forbid the tossing of rice because it's hard to clean up and it could actually harm birds who try to eat it. While birdseed has become more popular over the years, it has lost its novelty because more and more couples are using it. Here are some other nifty ways your guests can shower you as you depart your wedding:

- blow bubbles
- ring bells
- toss candy (wrapped candy like Hershey's kisses works best) as a way of wishing a sweet life together
- throw flower petals
- release butterflies
- throw dried-flower potpourri
- light sparklers as you leave
- throw streamers (think of the ones people throw as they're leaving on a cruise ship)
- literally shower the couple with sprays from water pistols (obviously, only an option if you don't care about getting wet in your wedding attire)

I Do Data

According to a 1999 Wedding Trends Survey by *Bridal Guide* magazine, 87 percent of couples keep a guest book from their wedding.

Your Way or No Way

While the logistics of planning your reception may overshadow your ceremony, it's important to keep in mind that the ceremony is actually the more important event of the two. After all, it's when you and your beloved will become husband and wife. Where and how you get married, however, will say a lot about who the two of you are both as individuals and as a couple. Therefore, trying to make your ceremony personal and reflective of your personalities is key in having your wedding your way. Here are some other points about the ceremony to keep in mind:

🌿 If you're going to write your own vows, make sure you give yourself enough time to not only pen them but also to run your written words by those who can give you honest opinions of how your vows sound. Plus, if you're having a religious leader doing your ceremony, it is only right to run your self-scripted vows by him or her.

🌿 When planning a ceremony as an interfaith couple, you need to be sensitive to one another's needs as far as representing both religions at your wedding. You need to figure out if you're going to have a truly interfaith ceremony, for example, with a pastor and rabbi present, or whether it would be better to go with a simple civil ceremony. What if you want a religious ceremony? You could have a ceremony that represents only one of your faiths, or you could get married in an ecumenical house of worship, such as the Unitarian Universalist church. Just make sure you talk your religious issues out long before you book your wedding date. The key to having a successful interfaith marriage is talking openly about how each of your religions is going to factor into the new life you're starting together.

7

RADICAL RECEPTIONS

Callie and Mike are self-professed Anglophiles who are getting married. Their obsession with all things British, however, happened long before the two became an item. Callie studied at the University of Glasgow in Scotland and fell in love with the British Isles during her time abroad. Mike vacationed in Scotland and England once and then couldn't wait to return. Their shared interest in the United Kingdom was one of the things that brought Callie and Mike together.

Their love affair with our neighbors across the pond has continued in their courtship. For Callie and Mike, who live in Hoboken, New Jersey, there's nothing as sweet as going to afternoon tea at one of New York City's tony hotels. "Mike recently bought me a gift of a book about tea in New York. It's my goal to hit all the hotels for afternoon tea," says Callie. "Recently, we went to The Mark Hotel for chocolate tea, one of their specialties. They serve all sorts of wonderful chocolate sweets, in addi-

I Do Data

According to a 1999 Wedding Trends
Survey by *Bridal Guide* magazine, couples
do the following at their wedding
receptions:

- 95 percent feed the wedding cake to
  each other
- 93 percent cut the wedding cake
  together
- 87 toss the bouquet and 84 percent
  toss the garter
- 81 percent have a champagne toast
  given by the best man
- 78 percent have a first dance with
  their parents

tion to normal tea fare. We've also gone to the Waldorf-Astoria and The Plaza." Now that Callie and Mike are planning their wedding, does it surprise you that they are keeping their favorite pastime in mind? At Callie and Mike's wedding reception, they will forego the traditional sit-down dinner and instead have an afternoon tea. "We love going for tea and thought it would be a great alternative to traditional wedding fare," Callie remarks. Instead of salmon and salad, Callie and Mike's guests will be dining on scones with clotted cream, tea sandwiches, cookies, and candies.

Callie and Mike's wedding celebration is a great example of a couple planning a reception that truly reflects who they are. If you want to give your guests the chance to experience something other than the standard cookie-cutter wedding reception, make sure you add some personal touches to your reception (as you will with your ceremony—see Chapter 6, "Creative Ceremonies"). Explains Callie, "I think some people in our family were a little disappointed that we decided against the whole dinner-and-dancing kind of wedding reception, but it didn't really fit our personalities."

I couldn't have said it better myself. In fact, infusing our personalities into our reception was one of the criteria Bill and I had when we planned our wedding reception, which occurred on our original wedding date. (If you've read ahead in the book, you'll already know that we eloped. But Bill and I liked our caterer and photographer so much and we wanted a chance to celebrate our getting married, so we kept the party part of our wedding and had a big bash in June as we'd originally planned.)

Bill and I are very laid-back people, and we wanted our reception to reflect that fact. At first, we were going to have our reception at a yacht club, but, besides not being big enough to accommodate all of our guests, we decided that a yacht club might be a bit too snooty for our tastes. We ended up having our reception in my grandfather's backyard. He lives on a large plot of land with gorgeous gardens and lots of shrubbery. We had our caterer bring in a tent, just in case it rained. (Note: if you're going to have an outdoor reception, *always* use a tent. You never know when Mother Nature may decide to rain on your party.) The caterer also brought tables, linens, chairs, china, silver, and the works. In keeping with the casual nature of our reception site, we couldn't possibly have a sit-down dinner that required eight forks and wines to match each of the courses. No, we wanted our guests to nosh on finger food. Now, which meal of the day has the most finger foods? Why, breakfast of course. So, we decided that our wedding reception would be a Sunday brunch. Our

I Do Data

The top four places to hold a wedding reception, so says the Association of Bridal Consultants, are:

- catering hall (31 percent)
- country club (20 percent)
- church or synagogue (19 percent)
- hotel (15 percent)

caterer arranged it so that guests could go to various food stations and have omelettes or Belgian waffles made to order (the only food requiring utensils). And, there were baskets and baskets of bagels, muffins, and fresh fruit.

Then there was the wedding cake. Or shall I say cakes. Bill and I decided to have a groom's cake; a Southern tradition, along with the wedding cake. Because Bill is of Italian descent and loves cheesecake, we had the caterer make an Italian cheesecake, which she topped with fresh blueberries. The sides of the cake were a work of art; they resembled an intricately woven basket in yellow and white. The wedding cake was a chocolate buttercream delight decorated with fresh flowers—simply amazing.

Traditions with a Twist

Instead of simply serving wedding cake, why not have your caterer make cupcakes? Have enough on hand to serve all your guests, and top each cupcake with its own cake topper.

Speaking of decorations, don't be afraid to have some fun with the cake topper. Susan and Mike, who wore sneakers to their wedding and held their reception in a children's museum, topped the groom's cake with a Barbie bride and a Ken groom. But Ken's head was shaved to reflect the groom's lack of hair on his own head. "My husband told me that he did not want a groom cake topper with hair, because it wouldn't match his own looks," recalls Susan, who obliged by giving Ken a cueball look. Callie and Mike purchased a cake topper from on-line auction site eBay. It's a vintage 1940s bride and groom that Callie describes as "so romantic and sweet looking, and so much nicer than the plastic cake toppers."

Culinary Delights

Has all this talk about scones and muffins got your mouth watering? Well, it should. You want your guests to nearly salivate over the food you serve at your wedding, and finding a caterer to create these culinary delights is easier than you think.

First, think back to each and every event you've been to where the food was to-die-for. Then, find out who the caterer was at each of those events and ask the person who organized the party for contact information. Personal references, even if they're your own taste buds, are the best way to find a caterer for your wedding.

I Do Data

According to the Society of American Florists, 38 percent of wedding receptions are buffet, 34 percent are sit-down dinners, and 28 percent serve only cake and punch.

Once you find someone who makes food you like to eat, have a meeting with him or her. Not only does this give you a chance to talk about your wedding and the ideas you have for the food you're going to serve, but you can see whether or not you click with this person and can afford his or her services.

Bill and I knew immediately that the first caterer we interviewed for our reception was the one we would hire. She immediately laughed at all of Bill's silly jokes (a good sign all around) and offered a few jokes of her own. What was supposed to be a thirty-minute "get to know you" meeting turned into an entire afternoon of eating (she served us zucchini bread and homemade chocolate-chip cookies), drinking (freshly squeezed lemonade), and an all-around good time. The caterer showed

⟪ NEWS YOU CAN USE: YOUR OWN VINTAGE ⟫

A great way to add a personal touch to the tables at your reception is to serve wine that appears to be a vintage made especially for the two of you. How do you accomplish this feat? By buying wine from vineyards that will personalize the labels on each of the bottles. For example, Chaddsford Winery in Chadds Ford, Pennsylvania, offers a variety of red, white, and blush wines with personalized labels. Windsor Vineyards in Sonoma, California, offers a similar program of labels with the couple's name, their wedding date, and up to three lines of an individualized message. While having personalized labels on your wine bottles is a neat way to add a unique element to your reception, it can be pricey. One bottle of the Chaddsford Winery Chardonnay for example, is $12.99. In addition, not every state in the Union allows alcohol to be shipped over state lines. Windsor Vineyards says it can ship to only twenty-two states, so first call to see if your state is one that allows wine to be ordered direct.

For more information on personalized wine bottles, contact each winery. Chaddsford Winery is at 610-388-6221 (cfwine@chaddsford.com), and Windsor Vineyards is at 800-333-9987 (www.windsorvineyards.com).

us album after album of the great food and gorgeous cakes she'd made for other weddings, and talked with us about how we could have the reception of our dreams within a budget we could afford. By the time we waddled back to our car, we knew she was the perfect person to cater our wedding. After calling other couples who had used her and hearing marvelous things about her, we were convinced we'd found the right caterer for the job.

Speaking of references, even if your caterer almost intoxicates you with delectable confections, as our caterer did with us at that first meeting, make sure you call other brides and grooms who have used the caterer's services. Ask specific questions like "Did the caterer show up on time?" and "Was the food as good as the caterer had promised?" and "Was the staff courteous and responsible?" As long as the overall review you get is positive, you can feel confident in crossing "Find Caterer" off your wedding to-do list.

Strike Up the Band

In keeping with the casual theme at our reception, Bill and I kept our entertainment casual as well. Instead of hiring a band or deejay (no need, since there wouldn't be any dancing), we took our compact-disc player, which can hold five CDs at a time, and set it up to provide our reception with all the music we needed. We selected our favorite albums

---

❧ Doing It Her Way ❧

"The colors for my wedding were green and white, and I was having a hard time coming up with a song for the bridesmaids and groomsmen to dance to. Finally, we decided to have the band play Kermit the Frog's song 'It's Not Easy Being Green.'"

—Julie, Bristol, Pennsylvania

("Deadicated" and the soundtrack from *When Harry Met Sally* are two that I recall), hit the "shuffle" button, and we were set with four hours of wonderful music.

Using a CD player is an extremely economical entertainment method and one that I know other brides and grooms have used. Take Emily and Martin, who got married and had their wedding reception in the backyard of their Milansville, Pennsylvania, home. They actually used the CD player as background music during the dinner hour at their reception. "We wanted quieter music that melded into the background," Emily recalls. Their selections included Van Morrison and Enya. "We set the player on random play, but in retrospect it would have been better to have played each CD from beginning to end," Emily adds. "There were some jarring juxtapositions I could have done without. Still, it was an inexpensive music solution."

Besides the CD player, Emily and Martin had a Dixieland band playing fun, upbeat music during the cocktail hour. They decided to use this combination of entertainment options not only for financial reasons but because it also seemed to make more sense. With people walking around and mingling, it seemed appropriate to have a band playing music that, in Emily's words, "would

1 Do Data

The average number of guests at a wedding reception is 192, according to an Association of Bridal Consultants survey.

get people tapping their feet regardless of their generation and musical preference." Then, at dinnertime when things were more mellow, Emily and Martin didn't want a band or deejay who would distract the guests during the meal. "Besides, we weren't much into the whole first dance, deejay stuff that blasts your ears out at most weddings," she adds.

And what are the British-loving Callie and Mike doing for entertainment at their wedding? Actually, something very un-British but nonetheless original: They are having a jazz trio.

There's no rule written anywhere that you have to have a full band or a deejay at your reception. Hire the kind of entertainment that fits with your wedding and who you are—not what you think you're supposed to do. However, if you decide that you'd like to go the traditional entertainment route, make sure you've actually heard the musicians or the maestro deejay in action before signing on the dotted line. You'd hate to book a so-called swing band based on their slick website and then have them spend the entire reception playing R&B tunes only. Again, friends' weddings and other special events with live entertainment are great venues for finding great talent. As always, check references and be sure that the bandleader or deejay you like and want at your wedding will be the one who shows up. Put his or her name on the contract so there's no confusion as to who has the job. (Many bands and deejays are represented by an agent or part of a co-op, so specifying who you want is the key to being satisfied with the entertainment you hire.) And make sure you go over what songs you want played and when. Understand that you can't dictate each and every song the band or deejay plays—flexibility to play what seems to work well with the crowd is what makes a great bandleader or deejay—but you can give him or her certain guidelines about inappropriate music (no Hanson or Marilyn Manson, for example).

Flowers, Centerpieces, and Decorations

With my in-the-backyard wedding reception, it would have been crazy to decorate the tables with elaborate centerpieces featuring wrought-iron candelabras and exotic flowers. They would have looked completely out of place. Instead, my centerpieces were very natural looking and simple. My mother, an accomplished gardener who designed the centerpieces, took grapevine wreaths and lightly wrapped them in lace. Then, she placed one wreath at the center of each table and inside the wreath's circle clustered clay flowerpots with freshly potted flowers. We chose brightly colored flowers in season, not only because they were less expensive than exotic blooms but also because they would look the healthiest. Our choices included pansies, petunias, and impatiens. We were able to get four or five flowerpots per table. Additionally, we used the flowerpots to line the walk leading up to the tent. All told, we had enough flowerpots on the tables and on the walks so that each guest who attended could take one home as a favor.

It seems my idea of using potted flowers as centerpieces was ahead of the trend. Nathaniel Shell, owner of Nathaniel's Flowers Etc. in Dallas, Texas, reports that of late he's been using fabric-wrapped flowerpots with flowers in them or plants as centerpieces, specifically topiaries, which the bride then gives to guests as gifts.

Some brides choose other kinds of centerpieces that double as favors. They find that clusters of something work well in this capacity. For example, I've heard of centerpieces of clusters of votive candles, and each guest takes a candle at the end of the evening. (It helps with cleanup, too!) I've also heard of a reception table having a cluster of small goldfish bowls on it, with real-live fish inside.

Centerpieces can also do the double-duty thing if they originated from the ceremony (flowers that decorated the pews can also be used to decorate the reception tables) or even from the rehearsal dinner from the night before. "If we use the centerpieces from the rehearsal dinner, we'll just add more flowers for the reception the next evening. That way they look a little different and it isn't such a big expense," says Shell. "Brides want more value for their money. Some of them ask if it's tacky to do double duty, and I assure them that it is not."

Shell says that flowers aren't the only items that can act as centerpieces. "We're doing more with fruit mixed into the centerpieces," he says. "We've gilded apples, pears, and grapes, placed them in a silver champagne bucket, and then embellished the arrangement with flowers. Fruit is cheaper than flowers, so it's a more cost-effective way to decorate." It's also a creative way to bring some significance to your centerpieces. Adds Shell, "Old traditions say that fruit is connected with fertility and good luck."

I Do Data

Only 2.5 percent of couples pay more than $2,000 on their flower arrangements. According to the Association of Bridal Consultants, the average cost for flowers at a wedding ranges from $200 to $500.

Picture This

When Michelle, a bride who lives in Chicago but grew up in New York, was planning her Long Island–based wedding, she kept seeing photographs, all by the same photographer, in multiple vendors' photo albums and on the walls of the various catering halls she visited. "Every single great photograph that I saw had this photographer's name on it," says Michelle, who went on to hire that photographer to shoot her wedding. Not only did the photographer create pictures that "blew me away," recalls Michelle, but she approached Michelle's wedding with a photo-

⇜ *Doing It Her Way* ⇝

"We had our photographer bring two crews with her to our wedding and reception. That way we had pictures both of my parents walking me down the aisle and of the audience's reaction. At the reception, if people were making a speech, one camera was capturing my husband and me and the speechmaker, and the other crew were able to get the looks on the faces of my friends." —*Michelle, Chicago, Illinois*

journalistic approach. This approach is similar to what documentary filmmakers use when they're making a film. They record what is going on without being intrusive in any way. With weddings, documentary—or photojournalistic-style—photography focuses more on capturing candids rather than posing everyone. It's a style that's catching on for obvious reasons: you don't have an obnoxious photographer constantly in your face.

The photographer I'd hired for my reception was one who used the photojournalistic style. I'd seen her in action at a few of my friends' weddings—or shall I say, I knew she was the photographer at those weddings. She was so quiet and unobtrusive that, as a guest, I wasn't really aware that she was there, except when the flashbulb went off. To see her in action was to think she was simply another guest. She was nicely dressed and walked around mingling. If you didn't know any better, you would have thought she wasn't doing her job. But then I saw the pictures from these various friends' weddings, and they were fantastic. Better yet, I

～❀ Doing It Her Way ❀～

"After founding the special events department at the public relations firm where I work and planning swanky soirees at upscale hotels and crazy cocktail parties at places like the Henry Ford Museum in Dearborn, Michigan, I was determined to have an original party of my own for my wedding reception. The Children's Museum of Virginia is located in my humble hometown, and it seemed like the perfect fit. It would be a unique location, and because almost every exhibit there is interactive, it would give my guests something to do besides the same old dinner and dancing.

"Of course, my husband-to-be was skeptical at first, but all it took was one visit and he was sold. At the reception, my handsome groom and I had our pictures taken at various exhibits throughout the museum—in a fire truck, on a police motorcycle, in a big chair (picture the kind Lily Tomlin used to sit in), on a pretend train, etc. It was such a blast! We cut the cake in front of the big drum set in the music section. Every guest was thoroughly thrilled at the reception, although the parents of the small children who attended are now kind of mad at us. They said we set a bad precedent. Every time they tell their children that they have to go to a wedding, the kids think they are going to a museum!"

—*Susan, Portsmouth, Virginia*

discovered her prices were incredibly reasonable, she didn't tie you down to any preset wedding album packages, and, if you wanted, she'd give you the negatives of your pictures so you could handle making reprints yourself. When it came time for me to plan my wedding and hire a photographer, there was no question who I was going to have capture our celebration.

As with any wedding vendor you'll consider hiring, seeing the photographer in action at a friend's wedding is the best way to get a sense of how this person works. However, getting a recommendation from someone whose opinion you respect is also a great way to find a wedding photographer. Just make sure you see his or her work before you book a date. And keep the following in mind: make sure the photographer shows you the pictures from at least one wedding he or she has shot, from start to finish. You don't want to see an album of "best of" shots. Any photographer, even an amateur, can get off a good shot here and there, but it takes a real professional to shoot an entire wedding and have the whole thing look good.

Your Way or No Way

One of the key ways to make your wedding your way is to carefully choose your reception locale and the food you'll serve. These factors, together with the decorations and the entertainment you provide, will create an atmosphere that should reflect who you are as a couple. Keep the following in mind as you start interviewing vendors and visiting sites for your reception:

❧ Make sure any caterer you're considering feeds you. No, I'm not saying this to be your surrogate Jewish or Italian mother who wants you to eat a little something. Think about it this way: since this caterer will be serving your family and friends food at your wedding, you'd better try his or her wares beforehand. If you like what you taste—and you like the caterer—plus you can afford him or her, then you will have found your caterer. But don't just go with someone because everyone else is using him. The caterer you hire should not only be a good chef but a nice person, too.

❧ Pick a method of entertainment that fits your reception. A formal dinner calls for a lot of dancing, and a full band or deejay will be your best bet for getting your guests out of their seats and onto the dance floor. However, a casual backyard brunch beckons a more mellow method of entertainment, such as a jazz trio or prerecorded music. Just as you wouldn't want to wear a casual white sundress to your cathedral wedding, you probably couldn't get away with using your personal CD player at a big hotel reception.

❧ Find a florist, if you're going to use one, who can suggest centerpieces and decorations that fit well with the reception environment. See if you can figure out a way to have your centerpieces double as favors, which will be a cost savings as well as a practicality for you in the end. You won't have to worry about buying your guests gifts, and the cleanup after your wedding will be a snap because everyone will take a centerpiece home.

🐚 Avoid in-your-face photographers. I'm a big fan of photographers who use the so-called photojournalistic or documentary style. Compared with traditional wedding photographers, they are less intrusive, often less expensive, and they produce good work. Don't try to save yourself money, however, by hiring a photographer who works as a photojournalist. One bride did this (she hired a news photographer with whom she worked at a newspaper), and while the pictures of her and her husband were great, there were barely any pictures of their guests. "He tended to stick to the center of the action, which was where my husband and I were," she told me, "but he never turned around and took pictures of anything or anyone else." Make sure the photographer you hire has experience with weddings and can show you a portfolio that takes your breath away. After all, that is the reaction you want to have when you get your own wedding photographs back. They should amaze you.

8

HOBBY HONEYMOONS

While my husband and I are hardly sports fanatics, before we had kids we would hit the links almost every weekend. In fact, I have a very special place in my heart for golf. Why? Soon after Bill and I became a couple, he gave me a gift of golf lessons for my birthday. Considering I'd never picked up a club in my life, I was a little taken aback by his gesture. But then he explained his reasoning: He loves to play golf, and because he loves me too, he wanted me to share the sport he loves most. In short, he didn't want me to become a golf widow.

Taking up golf together made a lot of sense since Bill and I approached sports from very different perspectives. Before we became a couple, I pursued very solitary sports—biking, in-line skating, and running. Bill preferred to ride a stationary bike he had parked in the middle of his living room. When we tried to combine our hobbies—Bill would ride his regular bike alongside me as I in-line skated in the park—

it just didn't work. Once we discovered that I liked golf, we knew we had found a way to spend time together and get some exercise (we always walked the course whenever possible).

I loved each and every one of our golf lessons (no, I didn't wear bright green pants to them, but I did invest in goofy-looking golf shoes), and after I got the hang of the swing, I couldn't wait to get out and play nine holes (I never developed the stamina for eighteen holes during that first year on the links). Every weekend when we got the chance, we would go out for a round of golf. The day of our ten-year high school reunion? Bill and I joined a bunch of our high school buddies on the local golf course for a game of nine holes. (We all showed up at the reunion that night with sunburned faces, but that's a whole other story

---

❧ *Doing It Their Way* ❧

"I didn't consider Kauai a 'hobby honeymoon,' although since we're both quite active and outdoorsy, it did offer us those opportunities. We kayaked, snorkeled, and did a hard-core, all-day hike up part of the Napali Coast. At the end of the day, some locals gave us the thumbs up as they passed, since, although we looked pretty gritty, we didn't look any worse for the wear. We also hiked to areas at the top of Waimea Canyon that took us through marsh and, at times, left us ankle-high in red dirt and clay sludge. We had a wonderful active time as the outdoor folks we are. The thought of laying around on a beach makes us both want to puke!"

—*Therese and Michael, San Jose, California*

about the importance of wearing sunblock.) The first sunny weekend of spring? We were out playing golf.

A year later, when Bill and I were engaged and planning our honeymoon, we knew we'd have to go someplace where we could pursue our new favorite sport together. We booked a week's honeymoon at The Buccaneer on St. Croix, which has an amazing golf course that winds throughout the resort's lush grounds. The front nine holes offered unparalleled views of the Caribbean Sea—at one hole, you tee off on a spit of land with crystal-clear blue water all around it. The back nine were surrounded by indigenous flora and fauna. We played golf every day, and it was the best vacation I'd ever taken. I'm so glad we planned a honeymoon around our hobby, and I would highly suggest it to anyone.

Planning a hobby honeymoon—whether you want to pursue your hobby every day of your trip like Bill and I did, or for only a few days of your honeymoon—is a great way to personalize your first vacation together as husband and wife. Sure, anyone can go to a resort somewhere and lay on the beach for a week (and if your hobby is sunbathing, then more power to you), but don't you think that you would get bored after awhile? Instead, why not plan a trip that incorporates the very activities and pastimes that perhaps caused you to meet and grow closer while you dated?

That's the criteria Shannon and Paul used when planning their honeymoon. The couple enjoy being active together, including skiing at various mountains around the United States. When they decided to have a skiing

I Do Data

Sixty-six percent of all honeymoons take place in the United States, according to the Association of Bridal Consultants.

honeymoon, "people thought it was odd," recalls Paul. "But to us, lying on the beach seems such a waste of time. It's also very unhealthy, whereas skiing is super exercise." Even though the couple had enjoyed skiing together in Colorado, they decided to honeymoon in Lake Tahoe. "Living in New Jersey, we occasionally went to Atlantic City to play roulette and blackjack," says Paul. "Lake Tahoe offered the complete package of skiing, hiking, fine dining, shows, and gambling." Paul and Shannon loved Lake Tahoe so much that they've decided to return for a repeat vacation for their fifth anniversary.

Putting together a honeymoon that revolves around your hobby is fairly simple, especially if you know what you'd like to do (like Paul and Shannon did with skiing) or where you want to go. Your two best resources are the Internet and a travel agent who specializes in honeymoons.

The Internet

"For many young couples, the Internet is the first source to turn to when planning a honeymoon. It's a niche-market world out there, and the Internet will help a couple find the perfect honeymoon that fits their special interests," says Susan Breslow Sardone, who holds the position of "Honeymoon Guide" at About.com (http://honeymoons.about.com). There is a lot of information to sort through, though. For example, a recent Yahoo search with the words "sports vacations" yielded more than 2,400 responses.

Once you find a site that falls into the category of the kind of trip you're planning, you'll often find links to other websites with similar information, making your research more multifaceted and farther reach-

---

❦ *Doing It Their Way* ❦

"Our honeymoon was planned and booked entirely through the Internet.
We extensively researched our chosen destinations (Bali and Hong Kong)
via the World Wide Web and found an excellent rate with nice extras at
the Ritz Carlton in Bali. We booked through balivillas.com for the Bali
portion of our trip, and then we used a Seattle-based company called
discountasiahotels.com, which offers luxury hotels at good rates, to book
our Hong Kong trip." *—Kelli and Scott, Houston, Texas*

---

ing. "Although every couple is different, some of the most appealing
special-interest categories for honeymoons I've seen on the Net are bicycle trips through Tuscany, barging through France, and walking tours of
Great Britain," Sardone says.

The Internet offers more than just a way to pinpoint a destination
you'd like to visit. "Many of the hotels have full-page color photos of the
rooms, the surroundings, etc., as well as photos and information about
the destination" on their websites, says Lisa Price, coauthor of *The Best
of Online Shopping: The Prices' Guide to Fast and Easy Shopping on the
Web* (Ballantine, 1999). This allows you to take a virtual walking tour of
a hotel or resort where you might stay, even before getting on a plane.

In addition, "the nature of the medium, with its combination of
commercial sites, personal sites, usenet groups, and chat capabilities,
helps couples form a reasonable opinion of where to go on their honey-

moon," Sardone says. "It's the digital version of going to an all-knowing travel agent plus asking the opinion of literally thousands of friends who are all interested in the same subject at the same time."

If you've decided on a specific island where you'd like to honeymoon, use the Internet to help you get the most up-to-date information on your chosen destination. If you're going to honeymoon in the Caribbean or South Seas, for example, "start with the official website for the island. You'll find it by using search engines. Use search words like the island's name, "visitor guide," and "official," suggests Paris Permenter, coauthor with John Begley of *Caribbean for Lovers* (Prima Publishing, 1997). (Note: don't assume that a website with the URL www.theisland-name.com is the island's official website. While researching this book, I pointed my web browser to www.bermuda.com, expecting to get the official website of Bermuda. Instead, I found a website about business opportunities in Bermuda.)

"These on-line tourist guides offer a good starting place on activities, accommodations, weather conditions, and the nitty-gritty details of travel," says Permenter (Permenter & Begley's *Caribbean for Lovers* is also a fabulous resource). "From there we suggest checking out unofficial websites devoted to a destination or to a particular sport, depending on what interests you."

Travel Agents

If you would prefer to have a travel agent do all the research for you, at least find one who specializes in the activity that you both like. "You'll find many travel agents identify their specialty in their ads," says Permenter. If you can't locate someone in your local newspaper or via the

⊰ News You Can Use: Honeymoon Insurance ⊱

During your honeymoon planning, when your travel agent suggests you purchase insurance, don't write off the suggestion as just another way your travel agent can jack up the cost of your honeymoon. It really does pay to buy an insurance policy that will cover cancellation of your trip. "Paying $49 per person to cover trip cancellation is really buying peace of mind," says Nancy Zebrick, owner of All-Destinations Travel, an agency that specializes in honeymoons. If you don't buy insurance but suddenly you can't go on your honeymoon because you have to go to a funeral or because you or your spouse became ill, then you will have forfeited the entire cost of your honeymoon.

Don't think that postponed honeymoons don't happen.

In researching this book, I heard about a groom who injured himself on a ski trip before his wedding and ended up spending seven weeks in the hospital while his punctured lung healed; a bride who fell during her wedding reception and broke her leg, which prevented her from going on her honeymoon; and a bride whose father died days before the wedding, which caused the couple to postpone their wedding and honeymoon altogether.

Web, call the American Society of Travel Agents (703-739-2782), which can put you in touch with agents with specialties that match your needs.

Another option is to find a travel agent who is hooked into the Internet and knows how to use it on clients' behalf. One website that blends

I Do Data

Couples spend approximately $3,200 on
their honeymoons, according to a 1999
Wedding Trends Survey by *Bridal Guide*
magazine.

the travel agent and Internet relation
particularly well is www.1travel.com,
which has links to hundreds of travel
agents who specialize in a variety of
vacations. Under "Sports Vacations"
alone, you'll find the following links:
adventure, biking, boating, diving-
snorkeling, fishing, golf, hiking-walking, horseback riding, hunting,
rafting-kayaking, skiing, sporting events, surfing, tennis, and trekking.
"We work with more than 450 travel experts to help people plan trips,"
says Sally Lewis, marketing director for 1travel.com.

For example, if it's your first time to go somewhere in the world (as
it is with many honeymoons), you want to be able to speak with experts
who live and breathe planning vacations to your destination. "We utilize
the travel community and the power of the Internet to connect people
with experts who can help them plan their ideal trip," says Lewis. What's
great about working with a company that specializes in travel to a certain area is they probably book a huge volume of travel, which allows
them to get extra bonuses that a regular travel agent may not get. "In
many cases, they'll pass those savings on to the consumer," adds Lewis.

Sardone of About.com adds, "I always counsel honeymooners to do
their research on the Web but then book their honeymoon through a reputable travel agent. When something goes wrong, such as a missed flight
or a lost bag, there's nothing like having a human to call to help solve the
problem."

Another way to approach researching your hobby honeymoon is to go
through companies you've used previously or know others have been
happy using. For example, when I was single, I went to Club Med in St.

Lucia. I signed up for Club Med's tennis clinic, and every morning just after the sun rose, I attended tennis class where I worked to perfect my serve, backhand, and volley. Had I been such an avid tennis player when Bill and I got married I would have suggested that we look into Club Med for our honeymoon. And, actually, we did, but for the golf angle we knew we both wanted. What Club Med had to offer didn't mesh with our requirements, but that doesn't mean the company wouldn't work for you.

Another well-known company that offers to-die-for active vacations is Backroads, a California company that puts together inn-to-inn itineraries in some of the most beautiful places in the world—California's wine country, Italy, and France, just to name a few. The beauty of a Backroads vacation is you follow *your* itinerary on *your* chosen self-propelled mode of transportation, be it a bicycle, in-line skates, or your own two feet. Mileage on each itinerary varies according to your fitness level and stamina. (On a bike trip you might ride less than fifteen miles or more than twenty-five miles per day, for instance.) On a Backroads trip you can get all the exercise you want or you can take it easy. (A van follows travelers and will shuttle anyone not up to biking, hiking, or skating the requisite miles that day.) In addition, you can plan a Backroads honeymoon to include all the activities you both like. For example, a six-day,

～ NEWS YOU CAN USE: PLAN AHEAD ～

Filofax suggests placing a "menstrual calendar" in your date book so you can chart your monthly cycle and prevent any unwelcome surprises on your wedding day or honeymoon.

I Do Data

According to the Association of Bridal
Consultants, the following are the top eight
honeymoon destinations:

1) Hawaii   5) Jamaica
2) Mexico   6) Canada
3) the Bahamas   7) the U.S. Virgin Islands
4) Europe   8) Bermuda

"multi-sport" trip to British Columbia includes biking, hiking, and kayaking.

Furthermore, if you and your future spouse are into specific sports, see if a trade organization affiliated with your favorite pastime can help you plan your honeymoon. The Diving Equipment and Marketing Association (DEMA), for example, has more than four hundred members who specialize in scuba diving travel opportunities. Honeymooners and other travelers can refer to DEMA's website at www.dema.org for a specific listing of these companies. One such company that you'll discover by visiting DEMA's website is Weaver's Dive & Travel Center in Boulder, Colorado, which organizes escorted diving trips to some of the world's best diving spots, including St. Lucia, Saba, and the Cayman Islands in the Caribbean and Palau and Fiji in the Pacific Islands. "We have had several honeymooners join us on our group trips to take advantage of our group rates and personalized service," says Steve Weaver, president of Weaver's Dive & Travel. Web-savvy travelers can check Weaver's website (www.weaversdive.com) to learn more about the itineraries on upcoming trips.

Go Where Your Hobby Is

If you're into a specific hobby or sport, you can plan your honeymoon based on areas of the country or the world that are well-known for that activity. For example, if you are wine enthusiasts, a honeymoon that took you on a tour of wineries in California's Napa and Sonoma Valleys or on Eastern Long Island, where there is a burgeoning wine industry, would be perfect.

If your heart is set on going to the Caribbean, find out which islands are known for the kinds of activities you like to do together. "Antigua and St. Martin are top choices for intermediate and advanced sailors, and St. Croix and St. John in the U.S. Virgin Islands are wonderful destinations for couples who like to snorkel," says Permenter. "Windsurfers love Aruba, and hikers should check out Jamaica and St. Lucia."

Here's another "for instance": you love to go antiquing in your spare time. Going on vacation in the Caribbean would probably be a major bore for you. But what about booking a week in the Poconos in eastern Pennsylvania? Sure, the advertisements you've seen in bridal magazines for the Poconos seem very kitschy, but the truth is that area of Pennsylvania is well-known for great antiquing. Nearby Bucks County (where I happen to live, so I'm completely biased) is also a hotbed of antiquing opportunities. You could easily spend each day of your honeymoon checking for great bargains—and maybe even end up on pbs's "Antiques Roadshow" one day with one of your honeymoon finds!

Along the lines of a shopping honeymoon, consider booking yourself on a Caribbean island that offers duty-

I Do Data

Only 9 percent of couples go on a cruise for their honeymoon, according to the Association of Bridal Consultants.

The average length of a honeymoon is nine days. And in that time period, according to the Association of Bridal Consultants, honeymooners will spend more of their money in and around the hotel than anywhere else on their honeymoon.

free shopping. Both the U.S. Virgin Islands and the Islands of the Bahamas are well known as duty-free shopping destinations. There you'll find good deals on liquor and jewelry, among other items.

If you decide that kayaking, or crocheting for that matter, is exactly what you want to do on your honeymoon, then go for it. Honeymoons are often once-in-a-lifetime trips and you should have a vacation that is tailor-made for the two of you. "An activity-filled honeymoon can offer honeymooners a chance to bond because, as with the new life together, they are working toward a common goal," adds Permenter. "Active honeymoons following the hustle and bustle of a wedding can also be a great stress reducer. And, for couples who don't yet have a sport they enjoy together, the honeymoon is a great time to learn."

So if you've always wanted to become the next Tiger Woods (or at least a reasonable facsimile of him) or to learn to drive a NASCAR automobile, plan a hobby honeymoon so that all your dreams can come true. Bon voyage.

⤷ NEWS YOU CAN USE: TRAVEL WARNINGS ⤶

No matter what kind of honeymoon you're planning, if you're going to be traveling outside of the United States, make sure you check with the U.S. State Department to see if any warnings have been posted about travel to certain countries. You can find current and past warnings about practically every country in the world at http://travel.state.gov/travel_warnings.html.

Your Way or No Way

A honeymoon really is a trip of a lifetime, so doesn't it make sense to plan your itinerary to include things you love to do together? Keep the following in mind when planning your hobby honeymoon:

❧ Use the Internet. What did brides and grooms do before the cyber-revolution? I can't imagine how limiting it must have been before the entire world opened up and allowed us to investigate it. Finding a place to go on your honeymoon never was easier.

❧ Use a travel agent who uses the Internet. Travel agents are obviously experts in the honeymoon field. An agent who knows how to use the Internet to the client's advantage is an *uber*-expert in my eyes. Not only are his or her research capabilities endless, but the Internet-savvy travel agent can probably pass along discounts that "regular" travel agents may not be able to.

❧ Go to a place that has things you like to do. Like to shop? Find a duty-free Caribbean island. Want to mountain climb? Check out our national parks. Are you a theater buff? Then look into honeymoons in big theater towns, like New York City or Toronto, Canada.

❦ 9 ❧

WEDDINGS AWAY

When Barbara and Barry of Westport, Connecticut, began planning their wedding, they realized they wanted their day to be like no other wedding they'd ever attended. "We'd been to weddings with two hundred people, and we just didn't want something that big," recalls Barbara, who could have planned an intimate ceremony and reception in her Connecticut home, but decided that her once-in-a-lifetime wedding should also be a once-in-a-lifetime event. So Barbara and Barry, who had once vacationed on St. Barthelemy (know as St. Barts; it's a big celebrity hangout) in the Caribbean, decided that this tiny, picturesque island was the perfect venue for their wedding. With forty-five guests in attendance, Barry and Barbara became husband and wife during a poolside ceremony at the Guanahani resort.

What made their wedding special was not only the location but that their wedding turned into a quasi reunion of family and friends. "We got to spend five days with our guests, going snorkeling or hanging out on the

❧ *Doing It Her Way* ❧

"Because our family members live all over the United States and would have to travel to get to our wedding anyway, my husband, Fred, and I decided that we would have our wedding someplace wonderful so the traveling our guests did would be worth their while. Since we live in California, and Hawaii is easy to get to from there, we decided we would get married in Hawaii.

"We originally made plans to be married on Kauai, but then Hurricane Iniki hit the island about six weeks before our wedding and wiped out our plans. I can still remember sitting in front of the TV, watching news reports about Hurricane Iniki and crying. Fred told me that hurricanes hit the islands all the time and so not to worry. But when we saw a shot of the Hyatt, where our reception was going to be, and the whole first floor was underwater, we knew we would have to alter our plans. After a few frantic calls to our wedding planners (this is an example where they are worth their weight in gold), we were on a plane to Maui to plan a completely new wedding.

"Things sometimes happen for a reason, and Maui turned out to be an even better wedding location. Instead of getting married on a grassy knoll in Kauai (which was fine, but I didn't love it), we were able to arrange

beach," says Barbara. "Weddings come and go so quickly, but we got to celebrate our wedding for almost a week. It was the greatest thing we ever did."

to exchange our vows on the sixteenth hole of a Wailea golf course in Maui. It overlooked the ocean, and we were married just before sunset.

"One funny thing happened during the wedding: we were semi-buzzed by a tourist helicopter. I guess they thought it might have been someone famous getting married. Anyway, we all had a good laugh over that during the ceremony.

"Fred and I wore traditional leis during the ceremony. Mine was made from white flowers, and Fred's was made from green leaves. Later during the cocktail hour, we gave a lei to each of our fifty guests who'd flown in for the wedding. That was a big hit with everyone. Then, a guy dressed in traditional Hawaiian garb blew a conch shell to get everyone's attention. He lit a tiki torch above his head and led us all into the ballroom where we had dinner.

"We kept the Hawaii theme going in other aspects of the wedding, including with our cakes—at least one of the cakes: the groom's cake was shaped like a giant pineapple. Even our favors had a Hawaiian theme. We gave everyone Madame Pelei's tears (Madame Pelei is the volcano goddess)—handblown glass from Hawaii that can be used as Christmas tree ornaments. All in all, our wedding was perfect."

—*Katy, Woodside, California*

To many couples, getting married on an exotic island or in a resort location may seem well beyond possibility, not to mention beyond their purse strings. Yet, hundreds of couples each year plan weddings away.

Because traveling to a far-away destination isn't always feasible for friends and family, weddings away usually attract fewer guests. That, in turn, can help the bride and groom (or their family) spend less than the $16,000 couples normally spend on a traditional wedding, according to the Association of Bridal Consultants.

Weddings away also help you to stretch your wedding dollar further. Take my friends Laura and Don, for example. These two New York City professionals were lucky enough to budget $25,000 for their recent wedding—well above the national average for wedding spending, but far below what you can spend in New York City to get a decent wedding. Recalls Laura, "If we were going to have our wedding in Manhattan, we wouldn't have had any extras, like more than one choice for an entrée at the reception. But I didn't want to have just a basic wedding." Don and Laura started thinking about other places to hold their wedding, including the suburban towns near New York City where each grew up. But because Don's New Jersey boyhood town and the town where Laura grew up on Long Island are both within New York City's pricey metropolitan area, the couple discovered that these suburbs didn't offer many cost-cutting options either.

By chance they stumbled upon The Sagamore, a historic resort on Lake George, some five hours north of New York City. After visiting the resort and meeting with its wedding coordinator, Don and Laura decided to have their wedding there. For the same money they would have spent on a basic Manhattan wedding, they got a first-rate wedding at The Sagamore, which included a cocktail hour, appetizers, four entrée choices, and their wedding cake. "The places I'd looked at in New York City

~~≈ *Doing It Her Way* ≈~~

"My husband and I planned a wedding in San Francisco while I was living in Boston and he was living in Seattle. Having a wedding where everyone was an out-of-towner was a great experience. It was a special weekend away for ourselves and our guests. We were married the Saturday of a three-day weekend. We had 'open' bachelor/-ette parties on Thursday night (meaning anyone could attend), then we invited everyone for cocktails after our rehearsal on Friday. The day after our wedding, we had Sunday brunch and Sunday dinner with anyone who wanted to join us (we had 225 at the wedding and over 50 at both Sunday events).

"The logistics in planning this long-distance wedding were not as difficult as one might assume. I had lived in San Francisco for years and knew my way around. At one point, I spent four days in San Francisco meeting with caterers, florists, photographers, bakers, and dejays and had everything planned before I left.

"We blocked sixty rooms at a hotel on Fisherman's Wharf where both families and the majority of the guests stayed, making it yet another meeting place. Lastly, not having it in anyone's hometown allowed our parents to enjoy themselves and didn't make anyone play the role of host/hostess (in contrast to my sister-in-law's wedding, where her mother had eleven house guests and we prepared meals for the people for *three* days)."

—*Mary, Claremont, California*

were going to charge me extra for everything, including wedding cake," Laura adds. To top it off, Laura and Don were able to pass along the dollar-stretching benefits to their guests. Because they were booking a fairly large wedding (more than one hundred people), The Sagamore gave them a discount on room rates. And anyone who stayed at the resort could use its tennis courts, golf courses, and spas.

While Laura and Don's $25,000, one-hundred-person-plus wedding is a rarity for weddings away, it shows you how versatile you can be in

---

⊰ Doing It Their Way ⊱

"My husband and I had the hotel, caterer, etc., booked (but no deposits paid yet) when we realized that we didn't want a huge wedding after all. Instead, we went to Maui, where we had our honeymoon planned anyway, and got married at sunset on a cliff overlooking the ocean with our family and best friends as our witnesses. Our families stayed for a week of vacation with us on Maui, and then we went to the Big Island for our honeymoon. When we got back home, we had a luau reception at a local park. It was fun for everyone because they got to dress Hawaiian-style, it was very informal, and we had island dancers. Even though we spent $5,000 on the Hawaii wedding, which included our entire honeymoon, and $2,000 on the reception when we got home, that was still a lot less than what we would have spent on the wedding we had originally planned. Looking back, we wouldn't have done it any other way!"

—*Jennifer and Andrew, San Diego, California*

using your budget wisely. In general, it's not unheard of for a couple to be able to plan a to-die-for wedding on a white sand beach somewhere romantic and only spend $5,000—including their subsequent honeymoon at the resort. Better yet, any guests who are invited are expected to cover their own airfare and lodging, so that's two less expenses the couple has to incur.

From the guest's perspective, a wedding away can turn out to be a great deal. Many couples who plan faraway weddings let their guests know that they don't want any traditional gifts. Instead, they'd rather have the guest spend the money on getting to the wedding destination and participating in the celebration. For the guest, it's a forced vacation in a lovely locale, which is wonderful in and of itself. When Bill and I attended Laura and Don's wedding, we spent the preceding week vacationing in the Lake George area.

Not only does a wedding away make sense from a financial standpoint but it makes sense from a practical one as well. Chances are an engaged couple hails from two entirely different backgrounds—if not two separate coasts. They may have met in college or on the job and are likely to be living in a city far from where they grew up. Add to this the fact that about half of today's engaged couples have divorced parents who may no longer live in the same place where they raised their children. Planning a traditional hometown wedding isn't as simple as it used to be—if not downright impossible.

In addition, many first-time and subsequent brides and grooms are well-established in their careers. Therefore, they don't have a lot of time to plan a wedding. What's great about a wedding away at a resort is there's probably a person on staff whose sole responsibility is planning weddings for couples coming from out of town. The wedding coordinator at The Sagamore took care of Laura and Don's plans as did the coordinator at the Guanahani resort in St. Barts for Barbara and Barry's wedding.

If the resort you're targeting doesn't have its own consultant on staff (a rarity these days), you can work with a bridal consultant or travel agent who specializes in destination weddings, like Nancy Zebrick, owner of All Destinations Travel in Cherry Hill, New Jersey. Her specialty is putting together fabulous Caribbean weddings and honeymoons for couples from around the country who contact her through her website www.alltravel.com. Nancy plans hundreds of weddings away each year.

Lisa, a recent bride in Atlanta, couldn't have planned her wedding in Lake Como, Italy, if it weren't for the wedding planner she found who specialized in weddings abroad. How did Lisa find the company she used? The Internet. She hired this company because they happened to have extensive experience planning weddings in Italy. "We signed a contract for their assistance at a fee of $2,500," Lisa recalls. "We thought the price was high, but they were going to work out all the legal red tape for the wedding, locate and coordinate the ceremony and related activities, and also book all of our honeymoon travel." Lisa, who works in public relations and plans events, believes that even though she probably could have planned the whole thing herself, it was best to pay a little extra for someone to manage her wedding plans. "The time and effort to plan the wedding would have been extensive, and the language barrier was an issue," adds Lisa, who doesn't speak Italian. "The wedding planners had an Italian-speaking person on staff who handled most everything."

~❧ NEWS YOU CAN USE: PLAN VIA THE INTERNET ❧~

Thanks to the Internet, planning a wedding away is easier that it was in years gone by. For example, www.1travel.com, offers links to 43,000 properties worldwide (many offering wedding services) and more than 450 travel experts whose expertise ranges from Napa Valley to Nepal. This website even offers direct links to companies specializing in *planning* weddings away. There are a number of other websites that can help you make your wedding plans from afar. Use your favorite search engine to find them.

Before you send a company money, however, make sure you do your homework. Don't book and pay for any travel with any company on the Internet that doesn't come highly recommended from someone you know or that you haven't used personally. As you would with any company you use for your wedding, always check with the local Better Business Bureau or the state attorney general's office (where the company is located— not where you live) to see if there are any unresolved complaints against the company. Also, make sure that you use only secure websites when sending credit card information over the Internet. Secure sites provide encryption (scrambling of information) to cut down on the chances of hackers stealing credit card numbers.

Besides working with a wedding planner, what made Lisa's Italian wedding a reality was her ability to use the Internet to her advantage. Not only did it lead her to the wedding planners she hired, but it allowed her to "meet" the minister who would officiate at her ceremony. "The biggest hurdle was finding someone to officiate at our religious ceremony," says Lisa. (Lisa was told that she must have separate civil and religious ceremonies.) Her wedding planner couldn't find an officiant, so she started querying her friends who might have known an appropriate minister. "I asked a friend whose husband was a minister and a member of the Southern Baptist Convention, and within forty-eight hours I had the name of a minister who was working as a missionary and trying to start an English-language church in Milan." She E-mailed the minister, who agreed he would officiate at her ceremony. But the E-mail conversations didn't stop when the minister said "I will." "We actually did premarital counseling over the Internet with him as well," Lisa adds. "It was important to him to get to know us a little and to feel good about our decision to marry. So he drafted a few questions, and Gene and I answered them separately, and E-mailed them back to him. Then, we shared our answers with one another. It was a very sweet and romantic thing to do, and we loved it because many of our answers were remarkably similar."

In the end, Lisa and husband Gene got the wedding of their dreams. Their lakeside garden ceremony on Lake Como (attended by thirty-three friends from home) went off without a hitch.

From Lisa's experience alone, it's obvious why you'd want to work with an experienced consultant in planning a wedding away. Because the Caribbean is an extremely popular destination for weddings, many entrepreneurs have set up shop on the islands just to help Americans plan weddings. If you hire an outside company, like Lisa did, you can expect to pay a fee for the services. However, if you use a travel agent or go through your resort, the arrangement-making should be included in whatever price you're paying for accommodations. (If you're unsure, ask first.)

Not only have entrepreneurs benefited from Americans going away for their weddings, but so have the governments themselves. In many Caribbean countries, for example, the lure of American tourist dollars has become so attractive that a number of Caribbean countries have reduced their residency restrictions (if not obliterated them all together) for obtaining a marriage license. It used to be that you would have to fly to an island nation and spend one to two weeks there to fulfill the country's residency requirement before obtaining a marriage license. Now most islands will waive the residency requirement or request that you spend only twenty-four hours onshore before getting your marriage license. However, to get through the red tape more quickly (i.e., proving that you're an American citizen, that you've never been married or, if you have, you're legally divorced, etc.), you must fax your requisite documents to the island well in advance of your arrival. Having someone on the island to walk your paperwork through the appropriate channels for obtaining a marriage license is another reason why having a wedding coordinator makes sense.

If I haven't convinced you yet of why a wedding away is an attractive option, here's another piece of information to consider: The two most popular months for U.S. weddings are June and August—times when the weather is warm and predictably calm. If most couples plan a wedding on the eight or nine weekends occurring during these two months—and these popular weekends can be booked more than a year in advance—that doesn't leave a lot of options for couples with shorter engagement periods. However, there are plenty of places in the Western Hemisphere where it is warm and pleasant year-round, such as the Caribbean. By planning a wedding away in the tropics, a couple can expand their options for a warm-weather wedding from a few months out of the year to all twelve months.

Sometimes you end up planning a wedding away, but not in an exotic locale like Florence or the French West Indies. Instead, you may decide to get married in your hometown, and your simple wedding back home turns into a destination wedding without your planning it to be that way.

❧ Doing It Their Way ❧

"We decided to get married in Lake Tahoe because we spent so much of our youth up there. And we chose to get married on skis, because we love to ski and we wanted something original. Our wedding ended up being a ski weekend. All of our attendants met at noon on Friday to do a rehearsal on skis, and then our ceremony took place at 3:00 P.M. that day. Guests either skied to the ceremony site on the mountainside or were taken up to the plateau by a bus.

"After the ceremony, we rode the chairlift up with a JUST MARRIED sign on it—me in my dress and my husband in his tuxedo. It was a truly spectacular day, with two feet of fresh powder on the ground and clear skies all around. Afterward, everyone skied down to the lodge where we enjoyed hors d'oeuvres and drinks."

—*Susan and Jim, Silverthorne, Colorado*

Most of the guests whom you'll invite will have to travel to get to the wedding, even if it's to the little town in the middle of nowhere where you grew up. In order to make their time at your wedding enjoyable, you'll probably end up planning what's been coined the "weekend" wedding. But don't worry. Planning an itinerary for your guests can be a lot of fun. Consider the wedding that the following couple planned.

Kelli and Scott are busy media professionals in Houston. When they decided to get married, there was only one place they would consider becoming husband and wife: Kentucky, the bluegrass state, where they both grew up. They chose Louisville, where Kelli once lived, because it was the city that offered the most conveniences: an international airport, lots of hotels, and neat attractions.

They realized that a lot of people whom they were going to invite to their wedding fit into one of the two following categories: 1) they probably assumed that Kelli and Scott were getting married in Houston, where they live and work, and therefore would be surprised to discover they would be traveling to Louisville, Kentucky, for the wedding; or 2) they probably had never been to Louisville and might appreciate seeing a little bit of the city and its surrounding areas during their time in town for the wedding.

"Many of our guests live out of town and have never visited Kentucky. They are kind enough to dedicate vacation time and money to our special weekend, so we want to do everything we can to make the trip a little vacation for them," says Kelli, who went about planning an entire weekend's worth of activities for her guests.

As soon as she and Scott set the date, she let her friends and family know that they were in for more than just a wedding. And how did the couple notify everyone of their plans? With a Save the Date card, which brides and grooms traditionally send out when a wedding requires a lot of travel. These cards go out well in advance of invitations so guests can make necessary travel arrangements (See Chapter 5, "The Inside Scoop on Invitations" for more on Save the Date cards). The Save the Date card that Kelli and Scott sent out, however, was more than just a date printed on a card.

"We sent out an informal, information-packed newsletter to our guests, in advance of formal invitations, asking them to save the date," says Kelli. The newsletter starts off with this simple paragraph: "We hope this letter finds you enjoying the best of the New Year. As we reflect on the remarkable experiences of 1998 and look toward the millennium,

---

⚜ NEWS YOU CAN USE: LOVE IN LAKE TAHOE ⚜

When it comes to weddings away in North America, Lake Tahoe, on the border of California and Nevada, is one of the United States' most popular destinations. There were more than 15,000 weddings there last year, ranging from a slope-side ceremony after which guests threw snowballs (instead of rice) at the happy couple to a Western hoedown complete with bales of hay, tall-neck bottles of beer, and the Texas two-step. What attracts couples to Lake Tahoe is the fact that having a honeymoon there after the wedding is an attractive option. The Lake Tahoe Visitors Authority offers a free wedding-and-honeymoon planner to all prospective brides and grooms who call 800-AT-TAHOE or visit www.virtualtahoe.com.

we prepare for our most daring adventure . . . marriage. Please 'save the date' April 9–10 to celebrate with us back home in Kentucky."

The newsletter went on to list not only the basics (which airport to fly into and in what hotel they'd reserved a block of rooms), but also news about the engagement party they were having two months before the wedding as well as where they'd registered (Dillards and Ross-Simons). The newsletter also included the weekend's itinerary. On the Friday before the wedding, during the day, Kelli and Scott were first taking their guests on a tour of Prestonwood Farm, which raises thoroughbred horses, and then to a horse race after lunch. On Friday evening, they were having a rehearsal dinner and celebration at the Louisville Slugger museum. Finally, on Saturday, they were getting married. "Because we used the Internet extensively during our long-distance planning—and knew that our friends and family were tech savvy—we included helpful websites in our newsletter," says Kelli. Those websites included the stores where they had registered and the hotels where they had booked rooms.

❧ News You Can Use: Residency Requirements ❧

Since the Caribbean and Hawaii are the most popular exotic places for couples to tie the knot in a wedding away, the following are the requirements for getting married in either place. You'll notice from their marriage license fees and imposed waiting periods that some countries are more open to allowing nonnatives to get married on their soil (meaning the fees are affordable and the waiting period, if there is one, is manageable). If you don't want to live on a certain island for thirty days prior to your wedding, which some islands require (and while it may sound great on paper, it may be a bit of a bother if you have a job to go to or something like that), then choose to have a wedding away on an island with less severe restrictions. For example, on the Cayman Islands, there is no waiting period whatsoever for tying the knot. Better yet, hire a wedding coordinator or travel agent to handle the nitty-gritty details for you. You'll be glad you did.

The following information was accurate when this book went to press. Places may change their requirements from time to time, so make sure you check with the local tourist board before planning your wedding. Also, even though the Caribbean is a short plane ride away, the majority of Caribbean countries are foreign places to where it may or may not be safe to travel. Always check the United States State Department website before booking travel. It is at http://travel.state.gov/travel_warnings.html, and it can provide information about possible dangers American tourists may face when traveling abroad (and yes, even a place like Bermuda is considered abroad). For example, at the time of publication, Mexico, our seemingly innocuous neighbor to the south, was on the State Department's list of potentially perilous places to visit. For more information on traveling to the Caribbean in general, contact the Caribbean Tourism Organization at 80 Broad Street, 32nd Floor, New York, NY 10004; telephone 212-635-9530, fax 212-635-9511/-9512.

Anguilla

Marriage license fee: U.S.$284

Waiting period: two days

Documents required:

- passport or birth certificate and photo driver's license
- proof of divorce or death certificate, if applicable

Blood test: no

Antigua & Barbuda

Marriage license fee: U.S.$240

Waiting period: one day

Documents required:

- passport or birth certificate and additional photo ID
- proof of divorce or death certificate, if applicable

Blood test: no

Aruba

Call Tourist Board on-island, in advance, to schedule. Visit www.aruba.com for contact information.

Only religious ceremonies will be performed. Civil marriage is only allowed if one of the partners is a resident of Aruba or couple is legally married within their own country before arriving in Aruba.

Documents required:

- Jewish wedding: U.S. marriage certificate, verification of Judaism from home rabbi, and petition to the Aruba Jewish community

continued

- Christian wedding: U.S. marriage certificate
- Roman Catholic wedding: marriage permit from home priest, baptism certificate, and official form stating neither party was ever married in a church

Blood test: no

Bahamas

Marriage license fee: U.S.$40

Waiting period: twenty-four hours

Documents required:

- declaration certifying both parties are unmarried U.S. citizens sworn before a U.S. Consul at the American Embassy in Nassau, or marriage license obtained from Commissioner's Office for weddings on any Bahamas island outside of New Providence
- both parties must apply in person for the marriage license
- proof of arrival in the Bahamas
- passport or birth certificate and photo ID
- proof of divorce or death certificate, if applicable
- parental consent for parties under eighteen years of age

Blood test: no

Barbados

Marriage license fee: BDS$100 and $25 (in Barbados postage stamps)

Waiting period: none

Documents required:

- passport or birth certificate and airline tickets
- proof of divorce (in English) or death certificate, if applicable
- Roman Catholic weddings: the Catholic Church has additional requirements and

fees; contact the Bishop of Bridgetown for information

Blood test: no

Belize

Marriage license fee: U.S.$100

Waiting period: three days

Documents required:

- proof of citizenship
- proof of divorce or death certificate, if applicable

Blood test: no

Bermuda

Marriage license fee: U.S.$165

Waiting period: fourteen days

(*Note*: anyone wishing to be married in Bermuda must file a "Notice of Intended Marriage" form with the registrar general. Once the notice is received, it will be published in the local papers. Assuming there are no formal objections, the Registry will issue the license fourteen days later.)

Documents required:

- final divorce decree, if applicable

Blood test: no

Bonaire

Marriage license fee: U.S.$150

Waiting period: one week

(*Note*: to be married on Bonaire, either the bride or groom must write, at least two months in advance, to the governor of Bonaire, asking for permission to marry on the island. The letter must be accompanied by appropriate documents.)

Documents required:

- three passport photos of the bride and groom
- copies of passports
- proof of good conduct

continued

- proof of eligibility to marry (i.e., divorce papers, death certificates, proof of single status)

Blood test: no

British Virgin Islands

Marriage license fee: $110 in BVI postage stamps

Waiting period: three days

Documents required:

- passport or birth certificate and photo ID
- proof of divorce or death certificate, if applicable

Blood test: no

Cayman Islands

Marriage license fee: U.S.$200 (Nonresidents must obtain a marriage license from the Chief Secretaries Office. Two witnesses must be present at the ceremony.)

Waiting period: none

Documents required:

- proof of entry, i.e., Cayman Islands International Immigration Department Pink Slip or cruise ship boarding pass
- passport or birth certificate and photo ID
- proof of divorce or death certificate, if applicable
- letter from authorized officiating marriage officer

Blood test: no

Curaçao

Marriage license fee: U.S.$167

Waiting period: two days for residency, fourteen days to receive marriage license

Documents required:

- passport and birth certificate
- proof of divorce or death certificate, if applicable
- proof both parties are eligible for marriage

Blood test: no

Dominica

Marriage license fee: EC$300

Waiting period: two days

Documents required:

- birth certificate and proof of citizenship
- proof of divorce or death certificate, if applicable
- application form obtainable from the Ministry of Community Development

Blood test: no

Dominican Republic

Marriage license fee: U.S.$20

Waiting period: none

  (*Note*: U.S. citizens are required to write to the American Consulate in Santo Domingo, in advance of intended wedding date, requesting permission to marry [civil ceremony].)

Documents required:

- birth certificate

- proof of divorce or death certificate, if applicable
- parties must be at least eighteen years of age
- must bring a notarized letter from couple's local police department stating that they are in "good conduct/moral character"

Blood test: no

**French West Indies
(St. Barthelemy, St. Martin)**

Marriage license fee: none

Waiting period: none, but residency requirement is a must. One person in the couple must be a resident for thirty days (residency card is required) to be married here.

Documents required:

- birth certificate (or copy with raised seal)

continued

- certificate of good conduct (including certificate of single standing)
- residency card
- medical certificate issued within three months of event
- French translation of English language documents
- a *Bulletin de Marriage* and *"Livret de Famille"* are delivered at ceremony

Blood test: yes

Grenada

Marriage license fee: U.S.$15

Waiting period: three business days for residency; three to five business days to process applications

Documents required:

- passports and birth certificates of both parties
- deed poll if either party had a name change

- proof of divorce or death certificate, if applicable (Processing of marriage application may take slightly longer than two days if either partner is divorced.)
- proof of single status—letter from lawyer stating they have the legal right to get married
- affidavit of parental consent if either party is under twenty-one years old
- all documents must be submitted in English

Blood test: no

Hawaii

Marriage license fee: $50

Waiting period: none; however, both bride- and groom-to-be must appear at State Health Department office in Honolulu to apply in-person for a marriage license

Documents required:

- proof of age (i.e., birth certificate or driver's license)
- written permission from both parents, legal guardian, or family court if under age eighteen

Blood test: no

Jamaica

Marriage license fee: Jamaica$200

Waiting period: one day

Documents required:

- certified copy of birth certificate which includes father's name
- proof of divorce or certified copy of death certificate, if applicable
- documented parental consent if either party is under eighteen years old

Blood test: no

Martinique

Marriage license fee: varies

Waiting period: must be in residence at least one month prior to wedding day

Documents required:

- birth certificate with visa of Consulate translated in French
- premarital certificate translated in French
- document certifying single status translated in French
- valid passport

Blood test: no

Mexico

Marriage license fee: U.S.$200

Waiting period: two days

Documents required:

- passport and birth certificate
- a copy of tourist card or visa
- proof of divorce or death certificate, if applicable
- names, addresses, ages, nationalities, and tourist card numbers of four witnesses

continued

(*Note*: some cities require Mexican witnesses.)

Blood test: yes

Montserrat

Marriage license fee: varies

Waiting period: three days

Documents required:

- passports and birth certificates of both parties
- proof of divorce or death certificate, if applicable

Blood test: no

Puerto Rico

Marriage license fee: U.S.$2.00 (stamp fee for certified copy of license)

Waiting period: none

Documents required:

- ID card or passport (non-U.S. citizens must have passport)
- original birth certificate—for previously married brides only
- proof of divorce or death certificate, if applicable

- documented parental consent if either party is under twenty-one years old
- health certificate from a resident practitioner in Puerto Rico

Blood test: within ten days of wedding ceremony

St. Eustatius

Marriage license fee: varies

Waiting period: two weeks

Documents required:

- birth certificates
- proof of single status
- divorce papers, if applicable
- residence permit from the Immigration Department
- passport photos

Blood test: no

St. Kitts and Nevis

Marriage license fee: U.S.$80

Waiting period: two working days

Documents required:

- passport or birth certificate

- proof of divorce or death certificate, if applicable
- Roman Catholic wedding: if Catholic priest will perform ceremony, letter from home priest stating couple is unmarried
- Protestant wedding: if Anglican or other priest will perform ceremony, letter stating couple is known and unmarried

Blood test: no

St. Lucia

Marriage license fee: approximately U.S.$198

Waiting period: two days for residency requirements and two days to receive license

Documents required:

- change of name documents
- proof of divorce or death certificate, if applicable
- affidavit of one of the parties

- birth certificate or passport

Blood test: no

St. Maarten (Dutch)

Marriage license fee: varies

Waiting period: ten days to register at Office of Civil Registry, then three days to receive license. (*Note*: non-residents must receive special permission from the lieutenant governor. To do so, send a written request at least two months prior to intended wedding date.)

Documents required:

- passport, birth certificate, and airline tickets
- documented parental consent for those under age twenty-one
- proof of divorce or death certificate, if applicable
- all documents must be in Dutch or translated into

continued

Dutch by an official sworn
translator and notarized
Blood test: no

Trinidad and Tobago
Marriage license fee: TT$337.50
   payable in postage stamps
Waiting period: varies
Documents required:
   • proof of entry and intended
     exit, i.e., airline tickets
   • passport or driver's license
   • proof of single status
Blood test: no

Turks and Caicos
Marriage license fee: U.S.$50
Waiting period: two to three days
Documents required:
   • proof of divorce or death
     certificate of former spouse, if
     applicable
   • birth certificate and photo ID
     or valid passport
   • most churches require proof
     of membership

Blood test: no

U.S. Virgin Islands
Marriage license fee: U.S.$50
Waiting period: eight days
   (from receipt of notarized
   application)
Documents required:
   • Couple need not be on-island
     to submit application. Send a
     letter requesting a marriage
     license to the Territorial Court
     of the U.S.V.I. in St. Thomas or
     St. Croix. Letter accompanying
     application for marriage must
     state date of visit, length of
     stay, and preference of date if
     having ceremony performed
     by a judge (so an
     appointment can be made).
     Proof of divorce must also be
     supplied, if applicable.
Blood test: no

Your Way or No Way

There are many reasons why couples plan weddings away. They want to save money and so they decide to piggyback their wedding with their honeymoon. They want to limit the number of guests who will attend the wedding. They are looking for a once-in-a-lifetime wedding in a to-die-for location. If you're considering getting married in a faraway location, keep the following in mind:

❧ Give yourself plenty of time to plan. Planning a wedding takes a lot of time and patience, even when you're planning a wedding in your hometown. When you're doing your planning long-distance—and possibly in a foreign country—you have to give yourself even more time. Not every place in the world moves as quickly and efficiently as most North American locations, so what you would estimate to take just a few weeks to complete may actually take a few months.

❧ Use the Internet to your advantage. By using your search engines wisely, you should be able to track down information and plan a wedding anywhere in the world. But be a smart shopper when using any business you find on the Internet—or any-where else for that matter.

❧ Hire a wedding coordinator in the location where you are going to be married so he or she can deal with the day-to-day details of planning your wedding. Local peo-ple know the best ways to get through red tape, and because they plan weddings for a living, they have a lot more experience than you do. (Unless, of course, you're a wedding coordinator yourself. If so, you won't need anyone else's help, right?) If you're planning to have a wedding at a resort, see if there is someone on staff who can plan your wedding for you. Usually, resorts and hotels won't charge you extra for this service.

❦ Don't forget to send a Save the Date card as soon as you've set the date. By giving your guests a heads up, they can plan in advance to make all the necessary travel arrangements for your wedding.

❦ Work with a travel agent to help family and friends who will attend your wedding secure discounts on their travel arrangements. Unfortunately, the lone bride who is planning to tie the knot on an exotic isle doesn't have a lot of pull when it comes to airlines, car rental companies, and hotels. But a travel agent does. She brings those companies repeat business, especially if they treat her clients well, so they are more likely to give her better deals.

10

To Elope or Not to Elope: That Is the Question

When most people think of elopement, they imagine an affianced man ascending a ladder to his beloved's bedroom window. Let's get real: people who are planning to elope rarely escape on a ladder, unless, of course, it's in a Hollywood movie and the director is attempting to create an indelible image. Instead, the soon-to-be-wed who decide to bag the whole wedding to-do usually use planes, trains, and automobiles to go off to get hitched. For example, when my husband Bill and I eloped in 1992, we hopped in our Ford Escort and drove to the nearest justice of the peace. We weren't looking to create an incredibly romantic event by eloping. There were some very practical reasons for our elopement: we wanted to get married sooner rather than later because we loved each other, we were tired of dealing with all of the hassles that come with planning a wedding, and—because I was a self-employed person without health insurance—I could go on Bill's insurance policy earlier than planned.

Sometimes when wedding plans take on a life of their own, it may seem like eloping is your only option. And sometimes it is. Let me say for the record: there is nothing wrong with eloping just as there's nothing wrong with having a huge wedding. However, it isn't healthy to run off and tie the knot in Las Vegas because you want to get back at your mother (after she made her hundredth suggestion for a great caterer). "People marrying to spite their parents is unhealthy," says Elliot Cohan, a psychotherapist in Providence, Rhode Island. Along with wife, Beatty Cohan, a couple's therapist, he co-authored *For Better, for Worse, Forever: 10 Steps for Building a Lasting Relationship with the Man You Love* (Chandler House Press, 1999). "When a child is trying to get revenge on a parent by eloping, this is an immature expression of rebellion and that's not healthy."

Make sure you think long and hard about your decision to elope before acting. While eloping is exciting and empowering, it can be a letdown, too, especially if you've always dreamed of a fairy-tale wedding. "I have numerous clients who regret eloping," says Tina Tessina, Ph.D., a licensed family therapist in Long Beach, California, and author of *The Unofficial Guide to Dating . . . Again* (Macmillan, 1999). Try to think about how you'll feel five years down the road after you've eloped. Will you still feel good about your decision to forgo the big wedding? "You may regret not having those [wedding] memories to look back on," notes Tessina. Before you run off, think about whether or not you can put aside your adverse feelings about bridesmaid dresses and bands for however many more days, months, or weeks you have left before the big day and go through with your wedding as planned.

⫷ News You Can Use: Renewal Ceremonies ⫸

If you decide to elope but would like to experience some kind of special ceremony along with your basic "I dos," consider planning a vow-renewal ceremony during your honeymoon. This way you can do the traditional walk down the aisle, get all dressed up if you like, but not have the hassles associated with planning a traditional ceremony. A great place to do a unique renewal ceremony is in Tahiti, where you and your spouse will be treated like a royal bride and groom.

According to Tahiti Tourisme, a Tahitian wedding day starts with the bride being treated to a soothing massage and serenaded by her Tahitian bridesmaid. Meanwhile the groom is taken by boat to a *motu* (small islet) where he is painted with tattoos (temporary, of course) and given a crown of tropical leaves. The bride, wearing a flowered headpiece, is brought to the ceremony site via a rattan throne, carried by natives. Her groom arrives shortly thereafter from the *motu* in an outrigger canoe. Their traditional Tahitian wedding ceremony takes place on the beach. During the brief ceremony, the priest gives the bride and groom each a Tahitian name (as well as a Tahitian name for their first-born child). Afterward, the couple receives a Tahitian marriage certificate, which is printed on cloth parchment. Many couples celebrate the ceremony's completion by taking a sunset cruise. For more information about vow-renewal ceremonies in Tahiti, contact Tahiti Tourisme, 800-365-4949, tahitilax@earthlink.net or www.gototahiti.com.

Or have you become so unhappy with your wedding plans—and have tried to rectify all that is getting you down—that you have no other option to elopement besides calling off your engagement altogether? "Many families are so complicated today, with people in our society divorcing and marrying so frequently," adds Elliot, "that having a traditional wedding would make the couple and everyone else involved miserable." Elliot references a family where the bride's divorced parents hate each other so much that they can't stand to be in the same room, or the groom's mother won't be seen in public if the groom's father, to whom she is no longer married, shows up at the wedding with his new wife. With all this animosity floating around—and each parent's unwillingness to put aside his or her feelings for one day so that the engaged couple can enjoy their wedding—why wouldn't children with divorced parents want to elope? Understand that if your family has become so complicated that a wedding day filled with happiness and love is completely out of the question, then it's okay if you elope. Just understand what you're getting yourself into.

Why did my husband, Bill, and I elope? Well, straight dollars and sense, as far as health insurance premiums go. As I mentioned earlier, I was self-employed, and funding my own health insurance was extremely cost-prohibitive. By moving our wedding day up by seven months, I could go on Bill's insurance policy seven months earlier. Then there was the issue of our divorced parents. We both had them, and planning a wedding that pleased four separate sets of parents is an act of negotiation worthy of the United Nations' peacekeepers. And it was getting to the point where we felt like declaring war. The minutiae of wedding planning was quickly taking on a life of its own, and everything seemed to be getting out of control. Do we have a Viennese table? If so, must we really get chocolate-dipped strawberries along with the Linzer tortes? Or, in dealing with divorced parents, who should walk me down the aisle? Where would Bill and I seat our mothers and stepmothers without causing World War III? The turning point for Bill and me came on a nondescript weekend day when we were discussing with our mothers the color of the tablecloths at the reception. Without warning, a polite conversation comparing the merits of forest green versus meadow green tablecloths escalated into a shouting match. That night Bill and I joked, "Hey, we should just elope. Then we wouldn't have to care about stupid things like tablecloth colors." Suddenly, we realized the idea had merit, and after a few calls the next day to find out exactly where we could go to get married, we made an appointment with the justice of the peace at the Queens County Courthouse for the following Monday. Then we called our parents.

"What are you doing next Monday?" we each asked our mother and father.

"Why?" they each replied.

"We're going to get married."

"No, really, why are you asking about Monday?"

"Seriously, we're going to get married. We're eloping, but we want you to be there," we told our stunned parents. "But here's the deal: you can come if you promise to be on your best behavior. No fighting with your ex, no snide comments under your breath, just be there for us."

That next Monday, at 1:00 P.M., everyone showed up, and guess what? Everyone was on his or her best behavior. And our wedding day, a Monday in November (we all took off from work), turned out to be one of the happiest days of my life.

While Bill and I didn't have the wedding we'd planned for, we got what we wanted—a day to be married when everyone was on his or her best behavior. By giving up our plans for the big walk down the aisle, we also gave up our chance to have a big party. Or did we? The more we thought about it, the more we still wanted to have the big celebration to commemorate our getting married. So what did we do? We got rid of the ceremony but kept the reception on our original wedding date. Now, if anyone argued about the color of tablecloths, we could say, "Who cares? We're already married." We knew that when it came to planning the party, we were back in control, and that's what mattered.

Taking back control in wedding planning is one of the main reasons why couples elope, but it isn't the only one. Sometimes finances play a big part in a couple's decision to elope, such as the issue of paying for health insurance did in my situation. Overwhelming wedding costs may make a couple lean toward the option of eloping. For example, if the couple has decided that they will pay for the wedding themselves—and their parents refuse to cut down the guest list and to chip in funds—then the couple may be left with no other option but to elope.

Many times, couples of differing religious or ethnic backgrounds choose to elope to avoid any problems their "mixed" marriage might cause in planning a traditional wedding. That's the reason Eileen and Stuart of New York City decided to elope.

"Stuart's younger brother, Marc, had just gotten married a few months before we'd gotten engaged, and we watched the hell Marc and Robin went through in planning their wedding—and they're both Jewish," recalls Eileen, who is Catholic. "Stuart's mother insisted that Marc and Robin's wedding go the whole nine yards in being a proper Jewish wedding, from the *huppah* to a kosher reception. My future mother-in-law was meddling in every detail of Marc and Robin's wedding, and I just couldn't imagine going through that myself," Eileen says. When she and

Stuart decided to get married, "we knew planning a wedding would not be an enjoyable experience," Eileen recalls, so the two planned an elopement. They invited Marc and Robin as their witnesses along with one of Eileen's friends from college. The couple told their parents after the fact.

They drove to Eileen's parents' home in Connecticut, where the news was greeted warmly. The scene was quite the opposite at Stuart's parents' home. "My mother-in-law literally fell to the ground," Eileen recalls. "If Stuart hadn't caught her, she probably would have cracked her head open on the tiled floor." Despite Stuart's mother's dramatic response to the news of their wedding, "she's never expressed her real feelings for me, although I know I'm not the woman she would have chosen for her son to marry, mostly because I'm not Jewish." Nonetheless, in the years since their elopement, Stuart's mother has grown on Eileen. "When she's with me, she's genuinely affectionate," says Eileen, who holds no ill will toward her mother-in-law for preventing her from hav-

---

Marriage Memoirs

File this one under "Just Be Glad Your Dad Didn't React This Way to Your Elopement." According to Susan J. Gordon, author of *Wedding Days* (William Morrow and Co., 1998)—a book of inspiring wedding stories for every day of the year—when famed songwriter Irving Berlin eloped with his beloved, a young girl named Ellin Mackay, Ellin's father wasn't too happy. So he wrote her out of his will—and the potential of inheriting his $10 million fortune. Luckily, Irving's wedding present to Ellin was a valuable one—the copyright to his well-known song "Always." While it never earned Ellin and Irving $10 million, it did eventually bring in royalties in the $100,000 range.

❧ News You Can Use: Seeking Professional Help ❧

When Lauren, who lives in Pensacola, Florida, was planning her wedding, her divorced father kept refusing to cooperate with her wedding plans. "First he refused to sit near my mother during the ceremony, because he said he didn't want to be seen in public with her," recalls Lauren. "Then, he didn't want to contribute any money as he'd originally promised." According to Lauren, her father kept making suggestions that would make her wedding day comfortable for *him*, not her. "At one point he suggested I redo our seating arrangements at the church so there would be a 'buffer' row between him and his wife and my mother, which I thought was ludicrous," she adds. "Finally, I told him to just grow up or not show up at the wedding." At this point, Lauren recognized that the problems she was having with her father—and had been having since her parents divorced when she was in junior high school—were beyond her control. So she called in a professional therapist.

Getting an unbiased and professional person to help you work through any problems is a very healthy and mature way to survive wedding plans. And while you may automatically assume that your local parish priest or rabbi can help you work things out, psychotherapist Elliot Cohan isn't so sure. "My question is what kind of training has a priest had in marital counseling? Simply because they are there and perform marriages doesn't mean that they are sufficiently trained," he says. Cohan says you can call your local chapter of the American Medical Association or the National Association of Social Workers for a recommendation of licensed therapists in your area. Word of mouth from friends and family (if you're comfortable talking about your problems) is also a great resource.

Once you have a few names and numbers to consider, keep in mind that, according to Cohan, there are a number of criteria you should use in selecting a counselor.

- The counselor should have a minimum of a master's in social work or a master's in counseling.

- The counselor should have experience counseling couples in situations similar to yours. Just as you would interview a wedding photographer before hiring one, you should do the same with a therapist. Ask "How many pre-wedding cases have you counseled?" and "Was the therapy successful?" and "How long did the counseling last?" You want to hire someone with a lot of experience, a history of successful counseling, and who doesn't tell you that cases end up being counseled for years.

- The counselor's record with the Better Business Bureau should be clean. "Make sure you see if there are any complaints lodged against this practice," warns Cohan.

Lauren ended up finding a local therapist through her company's Employee Assistance Program, who told her that five meetings with her and her father should be sufficient to start working through the problems that were preventing Lauren from successfully planning her wedding. Once they reached the fifth session, they could reevaluate if they wanted

continued

to keep meeting. Unfortunately, Lauren and her dad never made it to the fifth session. Lauren's father never showed up for the third session. When the therapist called him, in Lauren's presence, to ask where he was, the father started accusing Lauren and the therapist of changing the appointment time and not notifying him. After hanging up the phone, the therapist turned to Lauren and told her, "Don't waste your money on any additional therapy. Your father is a very selfish man and he's never going to change," Lauren recalls. The therapist told her that if she decided to go through with a traditional wedding, she should do her wedding in a way that made her happy, not her father. "I really wanted to have the big wedding with everyone there," Lauren adds, "but in the end it was just too painful not to have my dad be there for me in the way I wanted him to be." So Lauren and her fiancé hopped a plane to Las Vegas and eloped. "I'm so glad we did. We spent the weekend enjoying being newlyweds, and I wouldn't want my wedding to have been any other way," she says.

ing the wedding of her dreams. "I don't regret the fact that we didn't get married with a big wedding. Getting married was still special for us, even if it was just city hall."

Difficult parents, like Stuart's and those who are divorced and don't know how to get along, can cause a couple to elope, as well. "My mom and dad are divorced, and I knew that if I invited both of them to my wedding, only one of them would show up," recalls Diana who eloped with her husband Mike to a bed-and-breakfast on the Maine coast. But it wasn't just the stress of having to choose which parent would attend her wedding that caused Diana to bring up with Mike the idea of eloping.

"We were living in Memphis at the time, and weddings are a big deal there," says Diana. Because Diana was raised in Chicago and Mike grew up in St. Louis—the couple met while working for separate Memphis media outlets—neither understood exactly what they were getting themselves into by deciding to have their nuptials in their adopted hometown. "People started listing all the things we're supposed to do in planning a Memphis wedding," recalls Diana. "There were an engagement party, numerous showers, the kinds of food we were supposed to serve, etc. Before I knew it, we were starting to hemorrhage money." The proverbial straw that broke the camel's back was when a friend mentioned to Diana that she had to have a groom's cake at her wedding. "Why do you have to have a groom's cake when you have a five-tier mountain of a wedding cake that people probably aren't going to eat anyway?" Diana recalls asking. "I said, 'That's it. I can't take this anymore.'" Diana called Mike, shared her feelings with him, and discovered he'd been feeling as overwhelmed as she had. "So I asked Mike, 'Where's your favorite place in the country?' and he said, 'The East Coast.' That night I went to the bookstore and bought every book I could find on East Coast bed-and-breakfasts." Diana was not going to go through with a massive Memphis wedding; instead she decided to find an idyllic bed-and-breakfast where she and Mike could escape to tie the knot.

And she did. Mike and Diana became man and wife at a Maine inn overlooking the Atlantic Ocean. "We invited no one. Our witnesses were other guests staying at the bed-and-breakfast," Diana recalls.

So as not to leave friends in a lurch about their sudden disappearance, Diana had printed and mailed engraved announcements that said, "By the time you have received this note, we will have eloped to Maine." The announcement went on to invite friends and family to join Mike and Diana at a small party in their honor one month later back in Memphis. None of the people who received Mike and Diana's elopement announcement were bitter toward the couple—not even their parents. "Instead, people sent us congratulatory telegrams, bouquets of flowers, and bottles of champagne," she recalls. "By eloping, our wedding day clearly became *our* day again."

Finally, some couples elope because of all the wedding horror stories they hear from their friends. "Every single person we ever knew who got married told us that if they could do it all over again, they would just elope," recalls David of Newton, Massachusetts. So when he and Lisa, who'd been dating for three years, decided to get married, they knew exactly what they were going to do: elope.

"Not only did we lack the patience to spend every day of a long engagement listening to horrible wedding bands, deciding who should sit at what table, and making bridesmaids spend hundreds of dollars buying ugly dresses and shoes," he says, "but we wanted to do something that was just for us. In all of this big event, the details and money of the wedding tend to overwhelm the actual marriage, which is far more important." The twist in David and Lisa's story is they didn't go through the motions of planning a big wedding and then run off to get hitched. From day one, they planned their elopement without telling anyone about it. In fact, they never even told anyone they'd gotten engaged. (David never bought Lisa an engagement ring, a sure tip off. Instead, they chose a diamond wedding band for Lisa to wear once they were married.) "If we had told people we were engaged but didn't want to set a

⚞ NEWS YOU CAN USE: ELOPE TO VEGAS ⚟

To most Americans, the quintessential place to elope to is Las Vegas, Nevada. It's no surprise that the city of bright lights has turned eloping into big business. First of all, any couple who wants to tie the knot there only needs to shell out $35 for a marriage license. No blood tests or twenty-four-hour waits are necessary. And, even on weekends and holidays, the Clark County Marriage License Bureau is open twenty-four hours a day. (All you need to get a marriage license here is proof of age, such as a passport or birth certificate.) And with more than fifty wedding chapels open for business—some with a drive-through wedding window, some that are available all hours of the day and night—it's no wonder the Las Vegas Convention and Visitors Association reports that nearly 8,400 weddings occur here every month. That means every day 280 people tie the knot—that's one wedding every five minutes and seventeen seconds—in Las Vegas. For more information about eloping to Las Vegas, call the Clark County Marriage License Bureau's recorded information line at 702-455-4415 or log on to www.lasvegas24hours.com.

date, the pressure to plan a traditional wedding would have begun," Mike adds.

Using the code phrase "vacation to Disney World," David and Lisa actually began to plan an elopement to Jamaica. (See Chapter 9 on "Weddings Away.") They had a travel agent research resorts where they could get married. "We found that Sandals offers a 'Weddingmoon' package where the resort would handle all the paperwork, find a judge or clergyman to perform the ceremony, and provide witnesses, a cake, and champagne for one price," David says.

Unlike most wedding days, David and Lisa's turned out to be incredibly stress free. "We woke up late, went kayaking and snorkeling, then lay on the beach for awhile. Then we went back to the room, changed, and got married," he says. Lisa wore an off-white summer dress and an Ann Taylor scarf, and David donned a sports jacket, tie, and khaki pants for their sunset nuptials in a seaside gazebo in a garden. "Incidentally, there were lots of weddings going on and we were the only ones who did not wear 'traditional' clothes like a tuxedo and bridal gown," says David. What went through David's and Lisa's minds as they exchanged vows? "We were alternately thinking how happy we were, how we had clearly made the right decision doing it our way, and," adds David, "that our families would kill us" when they found out. (They didn't.)

Your Way or No Way

Eloping is the ultimate way to take back control over your wedding. But before you run off to have Elvis marry you, make sure that a blue-suede "I Do" is what will make you happy. Here are some tips to make your elopement go your way:

🕊 First and foremost, make sure you're eloping for the right reasons—you love this person and want to get married without all the fanfare of a big wedding—and not the wrong reasons, such as spite. If you're unsure of your motivation, talk to a licensed marriage or couple's therapist.

🕊 Don't turn an elopement into another wedding to plan. Keep things simple. If you need to plan your secret nuptials down to the exact time of day you want to tie the knot, put down the phone or get off the Web browser (which you're using to search for quaint New England inns) and get thee to a justice of the peace. In less than fifteen minutes you'll be pronounced man and wife. No blood, sweat, or tears.

🕊 If you don't want to hurt your parents' or siblings' feelings, invite them to your elopement. That seems to contradict the idea of elopement, but you'll be happy you had your family there to share in the big day—and they'll be thrilled to have witnessed the event.

🕊 Let family and friends know of your intentions—after the fact. In other words, keep your mouth shut about your plans to elope, or every Tom, Dick, and Harriet will be sharing their opinions about your decision to go against tradition. A great way to get the word out after the fact is to have announcements printed to herald your union. That way, if you plan to have some sort of celebration down the road, you can let everyone know about it on the announcement. For example, when Bill and I eloped, we had an announcement printed letting people know we'd gotten married. Then at the end of the announcement we printed "A June celebration is planned." We sent these announcements to everyone we'd intended to invite to our original wedding, and we had a big party in June.

❦ Even if you decide to have a ho-hum justice of the peace ceremony, do something special for yourself. Order a bouquet of flowers. Buy a new suit. Make reservations at that fancy restaurant you've been dying to go to. By carrying flowers or going out for an elegant dinner, you'll have special, albeit simple, memories of your wedding day that you both can carry for the rest of your life together.

11

SECOND WEDDINGS
AND BEYOND

There is a great benefit to getting married again—be it your second or seventh time. You are able to approach your wedding plans with more wisdom and knowledge than the first-time bride. At your first wedding, you may have gone to the cookie-cutter catering hall and had the wedding that your mother always envisioned her daughter having. Now you're planning another wedding for yourself, and this time, you'll do it *your* way. Don't worry. This time around, planning your wedding will be a lot easier. Once you've been there and done that, as they say, you'll know what you definitely don't want to do (toss the garter? do a dollar dance?) and what you wished you'd done the first time around but your mother badgered you out of doing.

While there's nothing wrong with having a big blow-out bash to celebrate your second marriage (or whatever number you're on), sometimes it feels more personal when you do things on a smaller scale. And I know from interviewing countless couples of whom one or both of the partners had been married before that couples planning another wedding for themselves want the whole wedding—from ceremony to the last piece of wedding cake—to be personal.

Take Bob and Lisa. When they decided to get married, they faced an interesting situation. While Bob had been married before, Lisa hadn't. Together they had to come up with a wedding that fulfilled all of Lisa's fantasies yet took advantage of Bob's wisdom about that long walk down the aisle.

The wedding Bob planned with his first wife was something out of *The Godfather*. The wedding party was huge, his first wife spent thousands of dollars on an incredibly ornate (can you say gaudy?) gown, and their cathedral ceremony made Princess Diana's nuptials look downscale. Then there was a reception at a large Long Island country club where only the best of everything was served. There was caviar, champagne, filet mignon, you name it. One of the reasons that Bob and his first wife's wedding was so over the top was that it became a de facto business affair for Bob's future in-laws, well-known and well-connected business owners who had to keep up their image of opulence, even at their daughter's wedding.

While Bob and his first wife had spent more than a year planning their to-die-for wedding, unfortunately, their actual marriage lasted less than a year. A few years after his first marriage dissolved, Bob met Lisa, and he knew right away that he wanted to marry her. (Good guy. He knew how to get back in the saddle.) But he also knew that he didn't want to go through the whole shebang again just to get hitched. Lucky for Bob, after talking things out, he discovered that Lisa didn't want a big to-do of a wedding either. So together they planned a wedding that became very personal for them.

Bob and Lisa were married by a justice of the peace in a simple ceremony lasting less than ten minutes. Then they celebrated their marriage with a tented reception in a relative's backyard in Connecticut. They served an eclectic mix of foods that represented their personal preferences (Lisa insisted on hand-rolled sushi while Bob demanded they bring in gourmet pizza) to about one hundred of their family members and closest friends. While their wedding was anything but traditional, it was exactly what the two of them wanted.

Here's another story to consider: When Susan at fifty years old found herself planning her second wedding, she realized something from her first wedding bothered her. The walk down the aisle went so fast (and she was so nervous she couldn't focus on anything other than making it to the altar without falling down) that she never had time to appreciate the audience at her wedding and what expressions everyone had on their faces. This time around, she was going to do things differently. "I stopped along the way down the aisle and greeted people," Susan recalls. "I just wanted to see everyone before we got married."

1 Do Data

The Association of Bridal Consultants says older couples are more likely to get married after 6:00 P.M.

Involving the Kids

Besides ways to make a wedding personal, what often affects a couple's ideas as they put together their wedding plans is the presence of children. Whether both people have a house full of kids or only one person has one child, it is imperative that they consider their children's feelings as they put together their ceremony and reception.

"It's natural for children of the first marriage to feel shunted aside when mom or dad remarries. While the parent is immersed in the excitement of planning a wedding and getting ready to combine households with a new person, all the child often sees is that some stranger is moving in on his or her territory," warns Susan K. Perry, Ph.D., a social psychologist and author of *Fun Time, Family Time* (Avon, 1996).

⟞ *Doing It Her Way* ⟝

"When I remarried fifteen years ago, my two sons were ten and twelve years old. They knew my future husband, Stephen, for the year we'd been dating, but they were still a bit leery of him—of anyone new becoming a part of our family. We helped them make the transition by involving them in the wedding. We had my older son safeguard the ring for us by keeping it in his pocket until Stephen needed it. He took this responsibility very seriously. My younger son, the more reticent one, didn't want any public duty, but I had him stand up at the altar with us. In the end, I made sure that both boys were front and center in many of the wedding photos."

—*Susan, Los Angeles, California*

Tina Tessina, a licensed marriage counselor in California and author of *The Unofficial Guide to Dating . . . Again* (Macmillan, 1999) advises: "I think it's critical to include the children, no matter what their ages, in the wedding, if you want future family peace. If children sense that their wants and feelings don't count when a parent remarries, they can really react and make life extremely difficult for both the natural and step parents for years to come." Believe it or not, a parent can deeply wound a child by not showing him or her that even though the parent is marrying someone else, the parent still loves that child very much. "By involving your child in your wedding plans, you're showing him that he still matters a great deal to you," says Perry, who suggests involving your children in even the smallest details of your wedding plans. "Ask your child what kind of napkins he thinks would look best with the planned decor. See if your children would like you to serve soda or lemonade at the reception so there will be something there they would like to drink. Find out if there is any favorite song or piece of music that they'd like to have played at the ceremony or reception."

A great way to make your or your future spouse's child feel a part of the wedding is to have him or her be in the wedding itself. Maybe your daughter could be your maid of honor or your future husband's son could stand up for him as the best little man. When my dad got married again, I was invited to be a bridesmaid in the wedding, along with his new wife's two sisters, who happened to be close to my age. Being a part of that special day was very important to me and helped me feel close to my new stepmother.

If your children don't want to have a traditional job, such as standing up, you have two choices. You can have them not be in the wedding, which you can suggest with the caveat that if the children change their

---

⇠ *Doing It Her Way* ⇢

"The original plan was for my three daughters, ages nine, seven, and six, and my husband's seven-year-old niece to walk down the aisle and then sit in the first row of the synagogue. As I approached the *bimah*, however, there were the four of them, two on each side, standing on the steps. The cantor thought they were so cute on the steps that we let them stand up there for the entire ceremony." —*Ellen, East Setauket, New York*

---

minds later on and want to participate, that will be welcomed as much as their decision to sit it out. Or you can get creative.

There's no law that says that the people who stand up with you at the altar or under the *huppah* have to have a title, such as maid of honor. A recent bride with two preteen daughters decided to have them stand up with her when she got married. Neither daughter was into the bridesmaid thing and both were too old to be flower girls. So they simply stood with their mother at the altar during the wedding, all of them holding hands. They wanted everyone in the audience to see that they were a family before the wedding and that they would remain a family after the vows were said. In fact, during the recessional, the daughters walked back with their mother and her new husband, all of them side by side and holding hands. (Luckily, their church had a very wide aisle.)

When Stevanne and Ralph of Berkeley, California, got married, both were in their fifties and had three grown children between them. "Having the children be involved in the wedding was very important to us," says Stevanne. "Children are very much a part of our lives, and we wanted them to feel very much a part of our relationship. They had made the original adjustments to handle the divorces, and we wanted them to know that it is possible for people to find love again—especially even at our age."

Because two of the children are musically inclined and the third is a gifted writer, Stevanne and Ralph thought the best way to include the kids in the wedding was to have them do something involving their talents. One of Ralph's sons composed an original song, which he played on the piano during the ceremony, and his other son, the writer, penned a poem. "He just spoke from his heart," Stevanne recalls, "and we were very touched." Stevanne and her daughter decided they would sing together. They chose their favorite song "You Light Up My Life." "It's a song about waiting so long for someone to come into your life, and while we were singing, it dawned on us for the first time that the song was saying exactly what was happening to me," Stevanne remembers. "We started to cry, she got choked up, I gave her a hug, and then we finished the song."

Some parents believe that saying vows to their children is the best way to make the children feel the most involved in the new wedding.

Marriage Memoirs

Talk about getting the kids involved: when Maria married Georg von Trapp in 1927 (the couple from *The Sound of Music*), her future stepsons escorted her down the aisle, and Georg walked with his older daughters, according to Susan J. Gordon, author of *Wedding Days* (William Morrow and Co., 1998).

That's what Teresa and Greg of Salem, Virginia, did with Greg's son, Phillip, when they got married. "The pastor who conducted our ceremony helped us write the vows to Phillip after we approached her and told her that we wanted a special way of involving Phillip in the ceremony," Teresa recalls. During the ceremony, Greg and Teresa invited Phillip to join hands with them and the pastor as they said their vows, which started off, "We promise to give you a solid family foundation and strength to grow." Teresa notes, "Saying the vow was very important to us to establish a family with Phillip and to help him understand that this day means something to him as well." Teresa and Greg added to Phillip's being a part of the wedding by having the caterer make a cake just for him (it had a toy motorcycle as its cake topper since Phillip was into dirt bikes), but they could have easily gone as far as having Phillip do a first dance with his new stepmom or sit with them at the bride and groom's table. (Phillip chose to sit with his younger cousins instead. Can you blame him?)

⋙ Doing It Her Way ⋘

"My stepson was six when I married his father, and we involved him in our wedding in lots of ways. One of the most touching—and fun—things I did with my new stepson was dance with him at the reception. Since my husband's father was deceased, I danced with my stepson when I normally would have danced with my father-in-law."   —*Teresa, Salem, Virginia*

Your Way or No Way

While personalizing your wedding has been the theme throughout this book, nowhere is that concept more true than when it comes to subsequent weddings. Once you've gone around once with weddings, you know what you'd do differently the next time around.

Of course, you can personalize your wedding in any way that seems appropriate for who you are as a couple, from serving your favorite food at the reception to tying the knot in a place that means a lot to you both. Just remember: if you've got kids, make sure you involve them in the wedding and, obviously, the marriage that comes afterward. When you marry someone with kids—or if you yourself have kids and are marrying again—you've got to remember you are creating an entirely new family that comes complete with kids. If you don't involve your children in the wedding, you may not be able to live happily ever after as stepmom and stepdad.

APPENDIX A
GENERAL INFORMATION

Following is contact information for a handful of associations, organizations, and businesses that I've quoted and referenced throughout *Your Wedding Your Way* that you may wish to get more information from when planning your wedding.

After I Do Registry
972-490-4470
800-956-4436
www.afterido.com

All Destinations Travel
888-ALL-DEST
www.alltravel.com

Association of Bridal Consultants
200 Chestnutland Rd.
New Milford, CT 06776-2521
860-355-0464
Fax: 860-354-1404
E-mail: BridalAssn@aol.com

Backroads
800-462-2848
www.backroads.com

The Bridal Party
243 E. 82nd St.
New York, NY 10028
212-861-2318
www.weddingcentral
    .com/ny/bridalp/

Chaddsford Winery
632 Baltimore Pike
Chadds Ford, PA 19317
610-388-6221
E-mail: cfwine@chaddsford.com

DogGone newsletter
P.O. Box 651155
Vero Beach, FL 32965-1155
561-569-8434
www.doggonefun.com

Dovetail Institute for Interfaith
    Family Resources
775 Simon Greenwell Ln.
Boston, KY 40107
800-530-1596
E-mail: DI-IFR@bardstown.com

Filofax
800-345-6798
www.filofax-usa.com

The Home Depot
800-553-3199
www.homedepot.com

Lake Tahoe Visitors Authority
800-AT-TAHOE
www.virtualtahoe.com

Las Vegas Clark County Marriage
    License Bureau
702-455-4415
www.lasvegas24hours.com/visitor/
    vis_wedd.html

Nathaniel's Flowers of
    Distinction
11613 N. Central Expressway,
    106A
Dallas, TX 75243
888-889-8917 or 214-691-1286
www.themetro.com/nathaniels

The New York Aquarium
Event Marketing
Surf Ave. & W. 8th St.
Brooklyn, NY 11224
718-265-3427
www.nyaquarium.com

1travel.com
800-901-0600
www.1travel.com

The Pleasure of Your Company
2360 W. Joppa Rd.
Lutherville, MD 21093
410-823-3052

Ross-Simons
9 Ross-Simons Dr.
Cranston, RI 02920-4476
800-556-7376
www.ross-simons.com

Society of American Florists
1606 Duke St.
Alexandria, VA 22314
703-836-8700
Fax: 703-836-8705
www.aboutflowers.com

Tahiti Tourisme
800-365-4949
www.gototahiti.com

Target
800-800-8800
www.targetstores.com

Tati USA
475 5th Ave.
New York, NY 10017
800-839-8284 or 212-481-8284
www.tatiusa.com

U.S. State Department Travel
    Warnings
http://travel.state
    .gov/travel_warnings.html

Windsor Vineyards
800-333-9987
www.windsorvineyards.com

Appendix B
Travel and
Weddings Away

Following is contact information for United States and Canadian tourist offices listed in Chapter 9, "Weddings Away." I have tried to provide as much information as possible. When an island nation requires foreigners to secure written permission to get married on their land, I have provided the address to which you can write to get more information. If you are on-line, you can find links to many of these websites via my own website, www.weddingink.com.

Anguilla Tourist Board
www.anguilla-vacation.com

The Wescott Group
39 Monaton Dr.
Huntington Station, NY 11746

516-425-0900
Fax: 516-425-0903
E-mail: info@Wescott
-Group.com

**Antigua and Barbuda
  Department of Tourism**
www.antigua-barbuda.org

25 S.E. 2nd Ave., Ste. 300
Miami, FL 33131
305-381-6762
Fax: 305-381-7908

610 5th Ave., Ste. 311
New York, NY 10020
212-541-4117
Fax: 212-757-1607

60 St. Claire Ave. E, Ste. 304
Toronto, ON M4T 1N5
Canada
416-961-3085
Fax: 416-961-7218

Aruba Tourism Authority
www.aruba.com

1 Financial Plaza, Ste. 136
Ft. Lauderdale, FL 33394
954-767-6477
Fax: 954-767-0432
E-mail: ata.florida@toaruba.com

1101 Juniper St. NE, Ste. 1101
Atlanta, GA 30309
404-89-ARUBA
Fax: 404-873-2193
E-mail: ata.atlanta@toaruba.com

5901 N. Cicero, Ste. 301
Chicago, IL 60646
773-202-5054
Fax: 773-202-9293.
E-mail: ata.chicago@toaruba.com

1000 Harbor Blvd.
Weehawken, NJ 07087
201-330-0800 or 800-TO-ARUBA
Fax: 201-330-8757
E-mail: ata.newjersey
  @toaruba.com

12707 N. Freeway, Ste. 138
Houston, TX 77060
281-87-ARUBA
Fax: 281-872-7872
E-mail: ata.houston
  @toaruba.com

5875 Highway #7, Ste. 201
Woodbridge, ON L4L 1T9
Canada
905-264-3434
Fax: 905-264-3437

Bahamas Tourist Office
www.interknowledge
.com/Bahamas

3450 Wilshire Blvd., Ste. 208
Los Angeles, CA 90010
213-385-0033
Fax: 213-383-3966

1 Turnberry Pl.
19495 Biscayne Blvd., Ste. 242
Aventura, FL 33180
305-932-0051 or 305-937-0585
Fax: 305-682-8758

8600 W. Bryn Mawr Ave.,
   Ste. 820
Chicago, IL 60631
773-693-1500
Fax: 773-693-1114

150 E. 52nd St., 28th Fl. N.
New York, NY 10022
212-758-2777
Fax: 212-753-6531

World Trade Centre, Ste. 116
2050 Stemmons Freeway
P.O. Box 581408
Dallas, TX 75258
214-742-1886
Fax: 214-741-4118

121 Bloor St. E, Ste. 1101
Toronto, ON M4W 3M5
416-968-2999, or 800-677-3777
   (Canada only)
Fax: 416-968-6711

Barbados Tourism Authority
www.barbados.org

3440 Wiltshire Blvd., Ste. 1215
Los Angeles, CA 90010
213-380-2198, 213-380-2199, or
   800-221-9831
Fax: 213-384-2763
E-mail: btala@barbados.org

150 Alhambra Cir., Ste. 1270
Coral Gables, FL 33132
305-442-7471
Fax: 305-567-2844
Email: btamiami@barbados.org

800 2nd Ave.
New York, NY 10017
212-986-6516 or 800-221-9831
Fax: 212-573-9850

105 Adelaide St. W, Ste. 1010
Toronto, ON M5H 1P9
Canada
416-214-9880
Fax: 416-214 9882

Belize Tourism Board
www.travelbelize.org

New Central Bank Building,
   Level 2
Gabourel Ln.
P.O. Box 325
Belize City, Belize
011-501-2-31913 or 800-624-0686
Fax: 011-501-2-31943
Email: info@travelbelize.org

Bermuda Department of
   Tourism
www.bermudatourism.com

9715 Cypress Brook Rd.
Tampa, FL 33647
813-973-3898

245 Peachtree Center Ave. NE,
   Ste. 803
Atlanta, GA 30303
404-524-1541

2835 Aurora Ave., Ste. 115-135
Naperville, IL 60540
630-585-6918

44 School St., Ste. 1010
Boston, MA 02108
617-742-0405

205 E. 42nd St., 16th Fl.
New York, NY 10017
212-818-9800

1200 Bay St., Ste. 1004
Toronto, ON M5R 2A5
Canada
416-923-9600

Bermuda "Notice of Intended Marriage" Registrar General
Government Administration
  Building
30 Parliament St.
Hamilton HM 12
Bermuda
441-295-5151
Fax: 441-292-4568

Bonaire Goverment Tourism Office
www.bonaire.org

c/o Adams Unlimited
10 Rockefeller Plaza, Ste. 900
New York, NY 10020
212-956-5912, 800-BONAIRE
  (USA only), or 800-826-6247
  (Canada only)
Fax: 212-956-5913

For permission to marry in Bonaire write:
Lt. Governor R. Hart
Wilhelminaplein #1
Kralendijk, Bonaire
Netherlands Antilles
011-5997-5330
Fax: 011-5997-5100 or
  011-5997-8416

British Virgin Islands Tourist Board
www.bviwelcome.com

370 Lexington Ave., Ste. 1605
New York, NY 10017
212-696-0400
Fax: 212-949-8254
E-mail: bvitouristboard@worldnet
  .att.net

1804 Union St.
San Francisco, CA 94123
415-775-0344
Fax: 415-775-2554
E-mail: bvitbsfo@pacbell.net

Caribbean Tourism Organization
www.caribtourism.com

80 Broadway St., 32nd Fl.,
New York, NY 10004
212-635-9530
Fax: 212-635-9511 or 212-635-9512

Cayman Islands Department of Tourism
www.caymanislands.ky

420 Lexington Ave., Ste. 2733
New York, NY 10170
800-346-3313

Curacao Tourist Board
www.curacao-tourism.com

475 Park Ave. S, Ste. 2000
New York, NY 10016
800-270-3350
E-mail: ctdbny@ctdb.com

Dominica Tourist Office
www.dominica.dm

800 2nd Ave., Ste. 1802
New York, NY 10017
212-949-1711
Fax: 212-949-1714
E-mail: dominicany@msn.com

Dominican Republic Tourist Office
www.dominicana.com.do/english/

2355 Salzedo St., Ste. 305
Coral Gables, FL 33134
305-444-4592
Fax: 305-444-4845

2120 W. Concord Pl.
Chicago, IL 60647
773-252-2889
Fax: 773-279-1233

136 E. 57th St., Ste. 803
New York, NY 10022
212-588-1012 or 800-752-1151
Fax: 212-588-1015
E-mail: dr.info@ix.netcom.com

2980 Rue Crescent
Montreal, QC H3G 2B8
Canada
514-499-1918
Fax: 514-499-1393

Grenada Board of Tourism
www.grenada.org

800 2nd Ave., Ste. 400-K
New York, NY 10017
212-687-9554 or 800-927-9554
Fax: 212-573-9731
E-mail: gbt@caribsurf.com

To file for a marriage license in Hawaii contact:
Hawaii State Health Department
Kina u Hale
1250 Punchbowl St.
Honolulu, HI 96813
808-586-4545

Jamaica Tourist Board
www.jamaicatravel.com

500 N. Michigan Ave., Ste. 1030
Chicago, IL 60611
312-527-1296
Fax: 312-527-1472

801 2nd Ave., 20th Fl.
New York, NY 10017
212-856-9727
Fax: 212-856-9730

1 Eglinton Ave. E, Ste. 616
Toronto, ON M4P 3A1
Canada
416-482-7850
Fax: 416-482-1730

Martinique Promotion Bureau
www.martinique.org

c/o French Government
   Tourist Office
444 Madison Ave.
New York, NY 10022
800-391-4909
Fax: 212-838-7855
E-mail: martinique@nyo.com

**Mexican Government
Tourism Office
www.mexico-travel.com**

10100 Santa Monica Blvd.,
  Ste. 224
Los Angeles, CA 90067
310-203-8191
Fax: 310-203-8316

1911 Pennsylvania Ave. NW
Washington, DC 20006
202-728-1750
Fax: 202-728-1758

2333 Ponce de Leon Blvd.,
  Ste. 710
Coral Gables, FL 33134
305-443-9160
Fax: 305-443-1186

300 N. Michigan Ave., 4th Fl.
Chicago, IL 60601
312-606-9252
Fax: (312) 606-9012

450 Park Ave., Ste. 1401
New York, NY 10022
212-755-7261
Fax: 212-755-2874

2707 N. Loop W, Ste. 450
Houston, TX 77008
713-880-5153
Fax: 713-880-1833

999 W. Hastings St., Ste. 1610
Vancouver, BC V6C 1M3
Canada
604-669-2845 or 800-44-MEXICO
Fax: 604-669-3498

2 Bloor St. W, Ste. 1801
Toronto, ON, M4W 3E2
Canada
416-925-0704 or 800-44-MEXICO
Fax: 416-925-6061

1 Place Ville Marie, Ste. 1526
Montreal, QC, H3B 2B5
Canada
514-871-1052 or 800-44-MEXICO
Fax: 514-871-3825

Montserrat Tourist Information

c/o Caribbean Tourism
  Organization
80 Broadway St., 32nd Fl.
New York, NY 10004
212-635-9530
Fax: 212-635-9511

Puerto Rico Tourism Company
www.prtourism.com

3575 W. Cahuenga Blvd., Ste. 405
Los Angeles, CA 90068
800-866-STAR

901 Ponce de Leon Blvd., Ste. 101
Coral Gables, FL 33134
1-800-866-STAR

666 5th Ave., 15th Fl.
New York, NY 10103
800-866-STAR

St. Barths Office du Tourisme
www.st-barths.com

Quai General de Gaulle
Gustavia, 97133 Saint-Barthelemy
French West Indies
590-27-87-27
Fax: 590-27-74-47
E-mail: odtstbarth
   @francemultimedia.fr

St. Eustatius Tourist Office
www.turq.com/statia

P.O. Box 6322
Boca Raton, FL 33427
561-394-8580 or 800-722-2394
Fax: 561-394-4294
E-mail: statiatourism@juno.com

**St. Kitts and Nevis Tourism
   Office**
www.stkitts-nevis.com

414 E. 75th St., 5th Fl.
New York, NY 10021
212-535-1234 or 800-582-6208
Fax: 212-734-6511

365 Bay St., Ste. 806
Toronto, ON M5H 2V1
Canada
416-368-6707
Fax: 416-368-3934
Email: skbnevcan@sympatico.ca

St. Lucia Tourist Board
www.st-lucia.com

820 2nd Ave., 9th Fl.
New York, NY 10017
212-867-2950 or 800-456-3984
Fax: 212-867-2795

130 Spadina Ave., Ste. 703
Toronto, ON M3V 2L4
Canada
416-703-0141
Fax: 416-703-0181

St. Maarten Tourist Office
www.st-maarten.com

675 3rd Ave., Ste. 1806
New York, NY 10017
212-953-2084 or 800-786-2278
Fax: 212-953-2145

3300 Bloor St. W, Ste. 3120,
    Centre Tower
Toronto, ON M8X 2X3
Canada
416-236-1800
Fax: 416-233-9367

For weddings in St. Maarten write to:
The Lieutenant Governor
Government Administration
    Building
Clem Labega Square
Philipsburg, St. Maarten
Netherlands Antilles
Fax: 011-5995-24884

St. Martin Tourist Office
c/o French Government Tourist Office
www.st-martin.org

9454 Wilshire Blvd.
Beverly Hills, CA 90212
310-271-6665

645 N. Michigan Ave., Ste. 3360
Chicago, IL 60611
312-751-7800

30 St. Patrick St., Ste. 700
Toronto, ON M5T 3A3
Canada
416-593-6427

1981 Avenue McGill College, Ste. 490
Montreal, QC H3A 2W9
Canada
514-288-4264

Tourism and Industrial Development Company Trinidad and Tobago Limited
www.visittnt.com

P.O. Box 222
10-14 Philipps St.
Port-of-Spain, Trinidad
West Indies
868-623-6022 or 888-595-4TNT
Fax: 868-623-3848

Turks & Caicos Tourist Office
www.turksandcaicostourism.com

11645 Biscayne Blvd., Ste. 302
N. Miami, FL 33181
305-891-4117 or 800-241-0824
Fax: 305-891-7096

United States Virgin Islands Department of Tourism
www.usvi.org

3460 Wilshire Blvd., Ste. 412
Los Angeles, CA 90010
213-739-0138
Fax: 213-739-2005

444 N. Capital St. NW, Ste. 298
Washington, DC 20001
202-624-3590
Fax: 202-624-3594

2655 LeJeune Rd., Ste. 907
Coral Gables, FL 33134
305-442-7200
Fax: 305-445-9044

245 Peachtree Center Ave.,
Marquis One Tower, Ste. MB-05
Atlanta, GA 30303
404-688-0906
Fax: 404-525-1102

500 N. Michigan Ave., Ste. 2030
Chicago, IL 60611
312-670-8784
Fax: 312-670-8788

1270 Avenue of the Americas,
Ste. 2108
New York, NY 10020
212-332-2222
Fax: 212-332-2223

268 Ponce de Leon Ave., Ste. 1101
Hato Rey, PR 00918
787-763-3815
Fax: 787-763-3890

P.O. Box 4538 Christiansted
St. Croix, VI 00822
340-773-0495
Fax: 340-773-5074

P.O. Box 200 Cruz Bay
St. John, VI 00831
340-776-6450

P.O. Box 6400
St. Thomas, VI 00804
340-774-8784
Fax: 340-774-4390

3300 Bloor St. W, Ste. 3120,
Centre Tower
Toronto, ON M8X 2X3
Canada
416-233-1414
Fax: 416-233-9367

INDEX